Spend
All Your
Kisses,
Mr. Smith

BOOKS BY JACK SMITH

Spend All Your Kisses, Mr. Smith
The Big Orange
God and Mr. Gomez
Smith on Wry
Three Coins in the Birdbath

Spend All Your Kisses, Mr. Smith

Jack Smith

McGRAW-HILL BOOK COMPANY
New York   St. Louis   San Francisco
Düsseldorf   Mexico   Toronto

234567890 BPBP 78321098

Library of Congress Cataloging in Publication Data

Smith, Jack Clifford, 1916–
Spend all your kisses, Mr. Smith.
I. Title.
PS3569.M5375S65   811'.5'4   78-8647
ISBN 0-07-058987-9

For Gail and Jacqueline

CHAPTER ONE

Nobody knows when middle age begins; not even the doctors and psychologists. It is said to be a state of mind as much as a physical condition, and its victim may be quite well into it before he realizes he is into it at all.

I know exactly the day on which I found out that I had already made this momentous passage, and in fact was well into it: Friday, May 23, 1969, rather late in the afternoon.

My discovery was heralded by the sound of our younger son Doug's motorcycle varooming up the hill. My wife and I heard him stop in front of the house and started out to greet him. He was living at that time in Westwood, where he shared a pad with two other UCLA students, and we were delighted by his occasional visits home.

We heard his familiar voice—young, playful, exuberant—and a second voice, the voice of a young, playful and exuberant girl, but a stranger. It was the first time he had brought a female home on his motorcycle. Usually it was books.

We hurried outside. What we saw unnerved us for a moment. They both wore glossy plastic helmets, his red, hers blue, with plastic visors distorting their faces. They looked like humanoid beetles. He kicked out the parking stand and settled the motorcycle and helped her off. She pulled off her helmet and shook out her hair. It was shoulder-length; a light reddish brown.

She rolled her eyes and made a little theatrical gesture of dismay. "I have ruin my permanent," she sighed.

She wore a shapeless blue windbreaker and blue jeans and chic brown boots; but despite this camouflage I made two hasty observations: whoever she was, she was full-grown; and she spoke with a French accent. I had a feeling that events of which I had not even been aware had already gone past some point of no return.

We asked them to dinner and they stayed. The young woman's name was Jacqueline Joyeux, the Joyeux being French for "joyous." My sense of inevitability was deepened. Our son was half-French, his mother being the daughter of French immigrants, and it was not surprising that he would be attracted to a girl named Joyeux, perhaps fatally.

Her home was in Tours, and she had come to America, on her own, on a visitor's visa. To prolong her stay she had found work as a maid in a Beverly Hills home, which was of course illegal, and was rooming with a clutch of French girls similarly employed in domestic service. Our son, evidently, had serendipitously come upon this nest of nubile Gallic pigeons and soon cut Mademoiselle Joyeux from the flock. Where it would end one could only guess, and I already had.

While the women tidied up in the kitchen, getting acquainted in French, a language that excluded my son and me, we went down to the garage and began loading the motorcycle for their adventure. They were planning to drive up into the mountains to spend the weekend, cooking out and sleeping on the ground in sleeping bags. It was nothing for me to worry about. Doug was no novice. He had spent four summers in the Sierras as a packer, and he knew its moods and perils and its sanctuaries. Yet somehow I had a feeling that he wouldn't be perfectly safe this time.

I watched in wonder as the supplies vanished into the motorcycle's saddlebags. A dozen eggs, a slab of bacon, a loaf of bread, a sack of potatoes, and a large package wrapped in butcher's paper.

"What's that?" I asked.

"Stew meat."

"You're going to cook a stew up there?"

"Sure. Might put a squirrel in it." His summers in the mountains had caused him to talk like Gary Cooper.

He found two sleeping bags in the garage and loaded them on the motorcycle, one on either side, for balance. Indeed, the motorcycle was beginning to look like one of the mules he used to pack for a trek in the high back country.

"Why a dozen eggs?" I asked.

"Well," he said, calculating, "four each for breakfast. That's eight."

"Of course," I said, remembering the extraordinary appetites of youth, especially in the mountains. "Four each."

They decided to stay the night and get an early start. Mademoiselle Joyeux was given the privacy of our spare bedroom and our son slept on the couch in my den, an arrangement that was not contested.

"Well," I told Denny when we were alone, "it looks like she might be the one."

"Yes," she said, as if she had always known it.

We were all up early. Mademoiselle Joyeux was at home in the kitchen. She prepared breakfast with the skill to be expected of a French girl whose father, as she told us, was once a chef. I watched her make a four-egg omelet for Doug. "He always like four eggs for breakfast," she explained. It struck me as a strangely intimate piece of knowledge.

They were dressed and packed and ready to go and we

were outside to wave them off when Doug decided to look in the garage for his old fishing pole. "I might try some fly-casting," he said.

"You have a license?" I asked, glad to be given some question of legality and prudence that I dared to offer advice on.

"Oh," he said, "I forgot that."

The problem really was, it turned out, that he didn't have enough money to pay for a license. He hadn't cashed his paycheck. I happened to have a twenty-dollar bill.

"I don't know how you can cash a twenty-dollar bill in the mountains," I said, "but you'd better take it anyway "

He took the bill and folded it into a pocket, and I realized that my status had changed: I was now an accomplice in the escapade.

They put on their helmets, lowered their visors, waved goodbye and trundled off down the hill. Denny and I were left standing in the empty street. The thrum of the motorcycle died out, and suddenly it was very quiet. I felt middle-aged, and slightly square.

It was a long weekend. I read two novels and the Sunday paper. It was growing dark on Sunday evening when we heard the sound of the motorcycle laboring up the hill.

Everything had gone well enough. They had taken the motorcycle as far as they could, then packed into the wilderness six miles on foot. Mademoiselle Joyeux was footsore but unrepentant.

He fished in a pocket and brought out the twenty-dollar bill. "Sorry it's wet," he said. "We had to ford the river."

Later I laid the twenty out to dry. It hadn't been much use. I realized I was dealing with a whole new set of values.

We saw Mademoiselle Joyeux rather often that summer and fall, mostly on weekends when Doug brought her by on his motorcycle. We were pleased to have her about. Our older son, Curt, was off with the Air Force in Southeast Asia, and we missed him. She helped to fill the house.

Denny had a woman to talk to, in French, and I was entertained by Mademoiselle Joyeux's buoyancy, her vivacity, and her Gallic impertinence. She happily regarded me as the embodiment of everything the French deplored in the American character. I was an easy target. When we fenced, which was often enough that I rather felt myself always en garde, she usually won the point. Her tactics were to pink me with a saucy thrust, unprovoked, as I saw it; and then, when I parried, to withdraw behind our language barrier, looking quite innocent, as if *she* were the injured party. Was it *her* fault if I didn't understand English? Meanwhile she kept me at my distance by calling me Mr. Smith, which came out something like *Mistair Smees*.

Part of her difficulty in understanding me, I thought, was that Europeans never quite grasped the American character. Their judgments were too hasty and too clouded by the European experience. That was demonstrated rather clearly one Sunday when Doug came by with Mademoiselle Joyeux and they found me watching football on TV, as they had more than once before. We were into the National Football League season at the time, and an American would think nothing of finding another American in front of his picture tube of a Sunday morning.

"Mr. Smith," said Mademoiselle Joyeux that particular morning, "you do nozzing else?"

"What do you mean?"—I said—"I do nozzing else?" I did not mean to mock her, but her accent was contagious.

"Every time I come to your house," she said, "you watch football on TV. You do nozzing else?"

I explained that on weekdays I got in my car and drove over the freeway to work like any other good American. But since she had never quite understood what it was I did for a living, or why I was paid to do it, I knew she remained of the opinion that I really did nozzing else but watch football on TV.

I got the impression in those weeks that she was not trying to understand me so much as trying to design me, to make me fit some stereotype for the middle-aged American male, especially one she might be appraising as a possible father-in-law.

She finally placed me in a category, but I wasn't to know what it was until late in October, after Doug had dropped out of college, quit his job and left town on his motorcycle with a vague announcement that he was going to see America before he was drafted. He meant to go all the way to New York.

It was warm in Lotus Land, but we knew the rest of the continent might grow cold in October. We worried about him, racing across the icy plains and through the bleak small towns of America. I thought I knew what compelled him. He was on an identity search. He had come to a crisis, and he needed to be alone in some vast space, to detach himself from his familiars, to discover the face and feel of his native land, to cross his horizons, to take his measure against a wider landscape. I had been caught up in the same kind of odyssey. I had gone all the way to the South Seas and Australia; but I had come back, and I knew he would come back too.

But we could see that Mademoiselle Joyeux was baffled and perhaps hurt by what must seem to her an act of desertion. It was her crisis too. We did not presume to probe or interfere, but we fetched her over to our house one evening for dinner, hoping the familiar setting and the wine and candlelight would make her feel at home and restore her confidence.

We dined outside in the patio. Denny had prepared a

small French dinner, and Mademoiselle Joyeux had pitched
in as usual to help with the table and make the salad. I
started to open a bottle of champagne but thought better of
it. Champagne might be too ostentatious, might make it seem
that we needed too desperately to be cheered up. Instead I
chose a Vouvray from the Loire Valley in which Mademoiselle Joyeux had been born and raised.

It was a lovely dinner. The evening was balmy, as October evenings are in Los Angeles. The sunset lingered, and
when twilight came I turned on the light in my goldfish tank.
The graceful little fish, so quick and vivid, added life and
color to the scene, and we finished the wine by candlelight,
talking softly.

Whatever anxiety any of us might have felt about our
missing Galahad was muted in the conversation. Mademoiselle
Joyeux was amiable and piquant. She personified that excellent phrase of her country, *joie de vivre.*

Then suddenly she grew pensive. She leaned toward me
across the table, her eyes searching mine. "Mr. Smith," she
said, still having trouble with it, pronouncing it *Smees,* "do
you think your son will someday be like you?"

It was hardly a question I had anticipated. But I was
touched. She was still a child, of course. It was only natural
that she would be impressed by maturity. I thought about her
question. Would our son someday be like me? Well, what
young woman *wouldn't* want her mate to be kind and gentle,
with a certain urban polish, a modest affluence, a mixture of
dash and prudence, and beyond that, as the French would
says, *je ne sais quoi.*

"What do you mean, *mon cher?*" I said gently, hoping
the familiar French endearment would make her feel at home.

"You know, Mr. Smith," she said, "*bourgeois.*"

Bourgeois! I was shaken. *Me* bourgeois?

What did the word mean, anyway? I had never been

quite sure. Something to do with middle-class values and a banal life-style. And it probably meant something even less admirable in France.

"Bourgeois?" I said, hoping I sounded merely curious, rather than defensive.

Mademoiselle Joyeux looked uncomprehending. She turned to my wife. "What does your 'usban' say?"

"Bourgeois," my wife said. "I think he said bourgeois."

I tried to explain to Mademoiselle Joyeux. I was not bourgeois at all, as I understood the word. Perhaps she had judged me too hastily, on a superficial acquaintance. Or perhaps the word lost something in translation.

"I am sorry, Mr. Smith," she said, "if I say something wrong."

"You must not blame yourself, *mon cher*," I said gently, giving her my patient smile. "English is a very difficult language. More wine?"

We sat for a moment in silence, avoiding each other's eyes in the candlelight.

"Well," I said at last, "perhaps I'd better feed my gold-fish."

"Oh, good!" cried Mademoiselle Joyeux, clapping her hands.

"You enjoy that?"

"Oh, *oui!* Mr. Smith. It is z'most exciting moment of z'day at your 'ouse—when you feed z'goldfish."

It really was rather exciting, I realized. Goldfish were such primitive little monsters. You couldn't domesticate a goldfish the way you could a dog. It was unnerving how the ferocious little nippers thrashed about, half-crazed with hunger. It seemed to me quite ridiculous to think that a man who kept goldfish could be bourgeois.

I opened the champagne after all.

It wasn't until we had driven Mademoiselle Joyeux back

to her lodgings and were on the way home that my wife told me *mon cher* was the masculine form. I wondered how a man of urban polish could have reached middle age without knowing how to say "my dear" to a woman in French.

CHAPTER TWO

We knew Doug was all right when he phoned collect from New York City to ask if we could wire him some money— just a few dollars to make it home on. Once he was out of the city he could sleep off the road, so all he needed was enough for food and gasoline.

He had never been to New York before, and he was properly awed, like any other young American pilgrim. He had arrived without enough money for a room, but he had luckily met two girls in a Greenwich Village coffee house and they had put him up for the night.

"We needn't have worried about him," I told my wife. "He has a gift."

A week later he limped home on a sputtering motorcycle. He was dirty and bone-tired, but fulfilled, somehow; he seemed purged of whatever conflict had compelled him, and I sensed that he now was set on some new course.

So it was not surprising when he told us he and his friends were giving up their pad in Westwood. It had been a good arrangement: three young students living together in a yeasty sort of academic mulch. But such harmonies end. Now they were going their separate ways; not in anger, merely in acceptance of change. Doug came home with all his worldly effects in a rented truck.

"Can I put this stuff in the garage?" he asked. "Temporarily?"

"Why not?" I said, wondering what "temporarily" meant.

It was a formidable load. A great heavy green overstuffed sofa and chair, two desks, twin beds, bunk beds, bookcases, bureaus, odd chairs, and an enormous refrigerator.

"It seems like more than you started out with," I said.

"Yes. The other guys don't have any place to put things."

I was happy to provide a home, if only for a backwash of used furniture. But there was no room left for our Dodge. "We'll park it outside," I said. "Temporarily."

He had three large cartons stuffed with books. "Put them in the front bedroom," I suggested.

The front bedroom had been the boys' bedroom. My wife had turned it into a work and sewing room for herself. But it had soon become overstuffed. I opened the door cautiously. Sometimes things fell out on you. We squeezed in, edging around the ironing board and sewing table. There were piles of yardage and patterns on the bed. Books were stacked around the walls. They were mostly the fruits of book club memberships we had inherited from our older son when he went overseas. There was no room for them in the closets. The closets were jammed with eighteen years of precious memorabilia.

I picked through the books in the cartons from the truck. Elizabethan drama. The Greek plays. A history of Byzantium. Shaw, Galsworthy. Virginia Woolf. They were marked and dogeared.

I envied him: all those marvelous books, read or yet to be read. So they had really studied out there at Westwood, after all. I hefted a book on classic Greece. Maybe I could start all over, at the beginning. No. Too heavy. Too late.

We tumbled the books out of the cartons and got one

of the bookcases from the garage and found room for it. It might no longer be possible to iron or sew in the room. But however long "temporarily" might be, we could never move from the house. We had a trust.

"If they ever get married," I pointed out to Denny, "all this stuff will come in handy. It's like a dowry."

"Yes," she said. "I might even throw in a sewing machine and an ironing board."

He also brought a rocking chair and a world globe that stood three feet high. I put the globe in my den, but there was no room anywhere for the rocking chair. I didn't know what we were going to do with it until I got up early the next morning, in the dark, and went into the kitchen for a drink of cranberry juice. As I groped toward the refrigerator, something struck the instep of my right foot. My first thought was that some intruder had been waiting in the dark and had struck me with a pickax. It was excruciating. I screamed. I grabbed the wounded foot in both hands and began dancing about on one leg in the dark. Lights went on. My wife burst in.

"What happened?" she cried.

What had happened was that I had hit my foot on the wedge-shaped point of a rocker. She had put the rocker in the kitchen.

"I thought it looked quaint," she said.

The garage, of course, was wiped out by Doug's impedimenta. It looked like the loading dock at the Salvation Army Thrift Shop. There wasn't even room for my garden cart, much less the Dodge.

Our life situation, it occurred to me, was a kaleidoscope. We kept shaking the little bits of colored glass about until they fell into a pattern that was pleasing to us—one we could live with. Then someone came along and gave it a bump, and the pattern was lost, never to be put back again in quite the same way.

We were bumped again that week. For a month past, bulky packages had been coming in the mail from our son Curt in Thailand. He was "short," as they said in the service, and was sending things home ahead of himself. He wasn't due for two more weeks, though, when the phone rang.

"I have a collect call from Mr. Smith in San Francisco. Will you accept the charge?"

Less than two hours later I picked him up at Los Angeles International. He had thirty days' leave before reporting to a new base.

"I hope you can put me up," he said. "Temporarily."

"Sure, if you don't mind sleeping in a warehouse."

It took him a day to unwrap the trove of packages he had sent home in the previous months. He had always had an eye for things of value. There would be no trash among his souvenirs. He had bought me a fine bronze Buddha, with one hand raised as a symbol of learning, and his mother a silver necklace the color of a twilight moon.

We adjusted. I even made peace with the rocking chair. In the mornings I sat in it in the kitchen and had my coffee and read the paper. The kaleidoscopic pattern kept changing, but the symmetry was always there, waiting to reveal itself, if you looked for it.

Then we were bumped once more. Doug told us that he and Mademoiselle Joyeux were going to France so she could be home for Christmas, and he could meet her parents.

So "temporarily" meant a little longer yet.

What worried me most when Doug decided to go to Europe was that he might leave me to take care of his motorcycle.

He had hoped to sell it because he needed the money, and there was no sense in letting it depreciate in the garage with his other things. But he was frantically busy, tidying up his affairs before catching the train for New York, as they planned to do, and I had an uneasy feeling that the motorcycle would be mine.

He had given me a ride on it one morning when my car was in the garage and I had been dreading the hard walk down the hill to the bus line.

"I can drive you to work," he said. "Can you wait till I finish breakfast?"

He was having a cold leftover enchilada and a can of root beer.

"I envy you," I said.

"You mean my motorcycle?"

"No. Being able to eat a combination like that at this hour."

I put on my light gray suit with a blue button-down shirt and a blue and red foulard. I was uneasy about riding to work on the back of a motorcycle, and not only because our hill is steep and the freeway is dangerous. It was a question of image. I got my briefcase. "I'm ready," I said.

I was just climbing on the back of the motorcycle when Gribble came out of his house across the street to take his trash cans in.

"Morning," I called out, giving him a casual wave with my briefcase. My other arm was engaged in holding on. Gribble's mouth fell open, but no sound came out. Or if he said anything it was drowned out by the roar of the motor as we sped away.

Halfway down the hill we passed Dr. Reap in his new Rolls-Royce. He looked incredulous, the way he does every year when he looks at my annual chest X ray. He says my rib cage is so calcified it looks like a Christmas tree in the snow. I waved my briefcase.

On the freeway I had a sense of freedom, racing through space without the usual wrapping of pressed steel. I felt as a bee must feel, buzzing from flower to flower. I couldn't remember that I had ever been on a real motorcycle before. Odd that I should have escaped this common experience for so many years. As a boy I was not allowed to associate with young men who rode motorcycles, or young women, either, though in my day that opportunity rarely came along. Decent young women did not ride motorcycles, nor associate with boys who did.

In World War II, during my service with the Marine Air Corps, I drove a motor scooter twice a day between squadron headquarters and the post office hut, to pick up the mail or deliver the mail, but I never felt that this contributed in any direct way to winning the war.

On the freeway a motorcycle officer overtook us. He rode alongside, looking us over. I wondered if we were doing anything illegal. It wouldn't hurt to be friendly. I'd heard there was a camaraderie among cyclists on the road. I raised my briefcase in salute and nodded. The officer shook his head and slid on past us, weaving out of sight through the traffic.

Doug dropped me off in front of the paper. "So long," he shouted, and sped away.

"Peace," I said, and raised two fingers.

It had been an adventure. There was something to be said for motorcycles after all, and unless Detroit gave us smaller and better cars we would all be on two wheels. Maybe the freeways would be friendlier then. The moment a man encapsulated himself in an automobile he was isolated from society. All other men became his adversaries.

But whatever its virtues, the motorcycle wasn't my style. I had no further need for a macho image. A man with a button-down collar and a briefcase and gray hair looked ridiculous on a motorcycle. Besides, I would never voluntarily give up the comfort of my car. Comfort was one of the compensations, and I was beginning to look for compensations.

The week before Doug and Mademoiselle Joyeux were to leave I grew increasingly uneasy. He had driven the motorcycle too hard on his cross-country trip, and before he tried to sell it he wanted to give it an overhaul. For days its parts had been scattered over what was left of the floor space in the garage.

"You'll never get it back together," I predicted, thoroughly pessimistic.

"Don't worry," he said.

"I don't want to inherit that motorcycle."

"Don't worry. No problem."

Two days before he was scheduled to leave he got it running. It sounded good. He took off down the hill for a test. Half an hour later the phone rang.

"Well," he said, "I've got trouble."

We rented a trailer with a ramp and rolled the motorcycle up on the trailer. It was much too heavy to lift. He lashed it upright on the trailer. He may not have known how to fix an engine but he knew how to tie a knot.

We drove it to a motorcycle shop, and there it stayed, waiting its turn to be fixed. They were in no hurry. He signed the pink slip over to me. My worst fear had come true. I owned a motorcycle.

"What am I going to do with the damn thing?" I asked on the eve of his departure. My agitation was real.

"You won't have any trouble selling it."

"I don't know enough about it to sell it."

"Keep it. You might learn to like it."

"Never. I'm too old and too bourgeois."

"Plenty of older men ride motorcycles. Remember T. E. Lawrence? He's a hero of yours. He rode a motorcycle."

"Yes. Right up to the minute he died."

The day came and we saw them off on the train. In this age of the jet, I realized, there was something especially poignant about seeing someone off on a train. It seemed more as if they were really going away, a long way away. I hadn't seen anyone off on a train since the war.

Afterward my melancholy was deepened by the thought that I now owned a big powerful German motorcycle. It was an expensive model, and it was busted. God only knew how much it would cost to have it fixed, and whether I could ever sell it.

Oh well, I thought, perhaps one should never distrust fortune. What seemed only a stroke of bad luck might change a life for the better. The dull schoolboy inherited a copy of Shakespeare's sonnets and became a poet; an awkward lad got a baseball bat for Christmas and grew up to hit .300 for the Dodgers. Who could say what a motorcycle might do for me?

If I couldn't sell it, I'd have to master it. I didn't think it would be much harder than breaking a horse. My father had broken horses as a boy back in Illinois. Maybe something of that hardy strain was in my genes.

I did think I understood the mystique. A man must have a heightened sense of being and freedom, racing in the wind with the earth and the sky up there in front of him as big and beautiful as CinemaScope, roaring into unknown dawns.

Anyway, I thought, it would solve the Christmas problem. My wife and I could give each other his and hers crash helmets.

When football season was over, I moved my electric chair out of the living room. It was big and comfortable, having three positions from upright to almost supine, and could be made to heat up or vibrate at the push of a button.

On the other hand, it was ugly. My wife despised it. It was the color of seaweed and had the grace of a nineteenth-century dental chair.

It caught my eye one night, out of all proportion with everything else, trailing black cables that ran across the carpet and plugged into the wall, and I said to Denny, "I've got to get this chair out of here."

"Where will you put it?"

"I'll move it into my den."

"What about watching football?"

"The season's over."

"Thank God for that," she said.

The next night when I came home I found the chair already in the den. It wasn't an easy chair to move.

"Who moved the chair?" I asked Denny.

"I did," she said. She must have wanted to move it very much.

It worked out quite well in the den, and I found myself doing more reading. There was just one problem. In moving the chair Denny evidently had damaged its electronic system, because when I pushed the button nothing happened. Luckily Curt was still on leave. I didn't know exactly what he did in the Air Force; out of patriotic prudence I had never asked him. But I knew it had something to do with sophisticated electronic equipment. He had had a great deal of schooling in the electronics school at Biloxi and after that had risen rapidly in the noncommissioned ranks.

"I wonder," I asked him, "if you could take a look at my electric chair? It isn't working."

"What's it supposed to do?"

"It heats up," I explained, "and it vibrates."

"One system or two?"

"What?"

"Do you have a switch for heating and a switch for vibrating or does one switch operate both?"

"Oh, separate systems," I said. "You can either heat up or vibrate or both. It's quite sophisticated."

We went into the den to look at the chair. He tried the switches. The chair heated not; neither did it vibrate. He followed the cord to where it disappeared behind my couch. The couch hid the wall plug.

"You're sure," he said, "you've got it plugged in?"

Our eyes met.

"Do you really think I'm that dumb?" I said. "Not to have it plugged in?"

It was a crisis; a moment of truth. He smiled.

"No, I guess not," he said. "It's probably just a short somewhere. I'll check it out later."

That evening he asked a friend from his squadron over to dinner. He was also an electronics man. I told him about the chair. I thought I was entitled to a consultation. After all, I was a taxpayer.

"Electric chair?" he said.

"Yes. For watching football. When you sit in a chair three or four hours on end, sometimes two days in a row, you can get cold and tense. I imagine it's something like flying a bomber."

He nodded slowly over the top of his beer. I led him into the den. He stood back, studying the chair. He tipped it forward to look inside. His eyes followed the cord to the wall where it vanished behind the couch.

"You're sure, Mr. Smith," he said slowly, "that you—uh—have the cord plugged in?"

"You're kidding," I said. I gave him a pat on the shoulder and we all laughed.

"It's probably just a short somewhere," he said.

A day or two later I inadvertently kicked a pencil under the couch in the den and got Denny to help me tip the couch forward, away from the wall, to look for it. Suddenly I knew what was wrong with my chair.

"You never plugged it in," I pointed out.

"I merely *moved* it," she said. "I thought *you* would plug it in."

I plugged in the cables and got into the chair and pushed the buttons. Instantly I heard a purr. I began to vibrate; and in a minute I felt a warmth at my back. It was bliss.

As I sat there in the plastic embrace of the chair, vibrating and glowing, I decided to sell the motorcycle. Who needed a motorcycle when he had an electric chair?

CHAPTER THREE

When Curt's leave was up I drove him out to Norton Air Force Base to catch a plane for his new post. He was going to England. It was a piece of luck. His original assignment had been to a base in Turkey, a bleak station out in the boondocks where men never saw anything but airplanes and goats. No one else wanted it, so he had volunteered. Then at the last moment a call had come from a base near London for a man of his rating, and his orders were changed.

We would miss him, but I was pleased that he was going. I thought of England as the country of my roots: I had grown up in England, through Dickens, Stevenson, and Conan Doyle, though I had never in reality been there. World War II had taken me the other way. For Curt it would be like a holiday. The war was behind him. He would see the sceptered isle at government expense, and perhaps have time to go across the Channel for a night in Paris, as every young man should.

But there was a thread of melancholy in my thoughts as I drove back to Los Angeles. For the first time, both our sons would be far away.

A letter awaited me in the box at home, and my spirits rose. It was from Doug, and it was postmarked London. He and Mademoiselle Joyeux were staying with her family in the village of Saint-Cyr, just across the Loire from Tours, but they had gone to Paris and taken the boat train to London for a holiday.

"Today we walked," he wrote. "Westminster Abbey is one of the most exciting things I have ever seen. We found it by accident, really. It is right across the street from Big Ben, all in the most ornate English Gothic style.

"The continental cathedrals are empty, vast shells of architecture, but Westminster Abbey is filled like a subway with statues, graves, and memorials. Queen Elizabeth, Richard II, Edward VI, Cromwell, and, of course, the poets: Chaucer, Milton, Johnson, Goldsmith, Keats, Wordsworth, and many others. Kipling and many more were actually covered with chairs for the Sunday services.

"The apse of Westminster Hall has walls of carved stone, and is completely filled with carved wood tombs, all of such fine and delicate workmanship that if you had one square foot of it in your house you would think you had a great work of art. We saw a plaque that marked the spot where Sir Thomas More was condemned. Terrible effect on the imagination . . ."

It wasn't a long letter, considering all he must have had to tell, and the real message was where I had learned to look for it in letters from distant sons—in the last paragraph.

"By the way, I hope you can both come to France for the wedding . . ."

They were going to be married in the *mairie,* or town hall, of Saint-Cyr. They would stay on in France for a few weeks after the wedding, then come back to America to live. Mademoiselle Joyeux's visa problems would be over.

We had three weeks to get ready. It was a fine excitement. Denny had never been to France, never seen Paris nor the mountain villages from which her parents had come, one in the Pyrenees, one in the Alps. She had to get a passport, and of course some luggage and some clothes, and all the time I was deciding that I couldn't go.

I finally told her. She would have to go alone. I was simply too busy to get away. For one thing, the house we were building down in Baja California, on the Bahía de Santa Tomás, was very nearly finished, and I would have to be nearby to see it through.

And of course, I pointed out, someone would have to stay home to take care of the automobiles and the motorcycle and the dogs. I had not only my own car, but also her car and our older son's car and our younger son's motorcycle. I hadn't sold it yet, and it was taking up much of my days and giving me bad nights. Sometimes in the morning when I woke up I counted my responsibilities on my fingers, like a mother with too many children. Also, who would feed the cats and goldfish?

She protested. She wouldn't go either. After all, it was going to be only a brief civil ceremony in the village mayor's office, not a big thing in the Tours cathedral. But I knew she had to go. Her roots were there, and now her grandchildren would have roots there too. Besides, she had bought new white boots and a white leather coat with a silver mink collar for the trip, and I knew that nothing, but nothing, should keep her from going.

I saw her off at the airport. As we said goodbye she told me, "Don't forget to put the trash out Tuesday morning."

It may seem a trivial thing to say at such an emotional moment, but getting the trash out was vital. If we missed on Tuesdays, we wallowed in trash for a week.

After the plane left I wondered how to remind myself to put the trash out Tuesday morning. It had always been her job. She had to get up earlier than I did in the morning, to get to work on time, so it was only natural. The trash truck came at seven o'clock, and it waited for no man.

It was not an easy task. We always had two or three barrels full, and sometimes four or five, especially if we'd had a big week for junk mail. Some Tuesday mornings it was touch and go. She would get up too late or forget it was Tuesday, and suddenly we would hear that galvanizing clank and grind and realize the truck was bearing down on us.

From the bedroom I could hear the entire drama—the cry of dismay, the opening and slamming of doors, the dash for robe and slippers, the clanging of the garage door, the groaning of the barrels as she dragged them out over the sidewalk, the anguished shout to the trash men:

"Wait! Wait for us!"

Once or twice I had put the barrels out myself, in emergencies, but it wasn't a good idea. If you have a system, you ought to stick to it. It's no good improvising so early in the morning.

Over the weekend, after she left, I could see that we were going to have a big trash. Three times the wastebaskets filled up and had to be carried down to the garage and emptied into the barrels. On the third trip I got my idea. I took one of the empty barrels and dragged it up to the house and through the front door and stood it in the middle of the living room.

It worked well. Whenever I walked through the room I dropped my trash in the barrel. When the mail came Monday morning I opened it over the barrel, setting the bills and personal letters aside and dropping the junk in.

Esthetically, a trash barrel in the living room may be controversial; but it is functional, and it might be considered an amusing pop comment on our civilization.

When the alarm went off Tuesday morning it reminded me of Denny. She would be in her small hotel in Paris. I wondered if she had awakened that morning in the City of Light and heard a truck rumbling over the Rue Saint-Simon and jumped out of bed, shouting, *"Mon dieu!* It is the trash!"

Suddenly I was aware of a clanging and scraping in our own street. I jumped out of bed.

It was too late.

My decision to stay home was hard enough to make, but I hadn't foreseen how much pressure would be brought to bear on me to change my mind—not just from members of my own family, but from colleagues at the paper where I worked and from strangers. They tried reason, sentiment, and shame. I was accused of everything from simple meanness of spirit to social alienation and psychic disassociation. One woman I didn't know sent me a two-word postcard saying "Go, Jack."

I appreciated the interest and sentiment, but in the end a man must keep his own counsel. Only he himself knows the urgings of his heart, the nature of his motives and his inhibitions. Decision is a lonely business.

The next-to-the-last thing my wife said to me at the airport, as she was about to board her plane, was "Sure you won't change your mind?"

Oh, I wanted to go, all right. Except for the most urgent reasons I never miss a wedding to which I'm invited, though I will duck a funeral now and then. A wedding is a joyous rite. It is an honor to be invited and an act of cynicism as well as bad manners not to go. One might as well not care about the sunrise.

Some years back a young woman living in rural Indiana had written a letter to the *Post-Tribune* in nearby Gary, inviting me to her wedding. She had got the idea that I worked on that newspaper, which sometimes printed one of my pieces.

I thought it was quaint, a man living in Los Angeles being invited to a farm town in Indiana for the wedding of a girl he didn't know. The editor of my paper didn't think it was quaint at all.

"When a gentleman from the *Times* is invited to a lady's wedding," he said, "he goes."

I went. I flew to Chicago, took the electric train to Gary, and hired a car that got me to the church on time. There was a country breakfast afterward in the school gymnasium. I had never seen so much chicken. They must have decimated the chicken population of Indiana.

Yes, I thought, a wedding is a joyous occasion. And surely this one would be especially so. I pictured the wedding party climbing the steps of the little town hall. I could see my wife in her white boots and leather coat. How cold was it in France? Perhaps it would snow. I had never been to Tours, but I had read and heard that it was a beautiful and historic city. Mademoiselle Joyeux's parents would be there too, and her younger sister, Nanette. *Nanette*. I loved the name. Even our older son might be there, as best man. Surely he could get a pass for his brother's wedding and cross the Channel. The armed forces were civil about such things.

I wondered if everyone would cry. Yes, they would, I supposed. Except the two young men, of course. Young men didn't cry at weddings, did they? Only nice old bourgeois men were allowed to cry.

I wondered if Doug would get a haircut. He had looked a bit rough-hewn when he left. We had never quite civilized him since those summers he had spent packing mules in the mountains. As the twig is bent . . .

I supposed there would be a wedding breakfast afterwards, in some country inn, with much wine from the valley, and perhaps champagne. There would certainly be champagne if *I* was there. I really hated to miss the breakfast.

Within the week of Denny's departure a letter arrived on the stationery of the Hôtel Saint-Simon, 14 Rue Saint-

Simon, Paris. I was surprised to find a slight tremor in my hands as I tore it open. I read rapidly down through the familiar handwriting:

"... We walked around Notre-Dame last night and visited le Tour Eiffel, Rue Pigalle and Sacré-Coeur today. I'm finding the cold *cold,* but also bracing and exhilarating. Tomorrow we go first to the American Embassy, then the Champs-Élysées *et l'Arc du Triomphe et peut-être encore au* Tour Eiffel to go up on the elevator. Today there was a line waiting at least ten times as long as the one for *Midnight Cowboy....*

"And the people! I think I am more fascinated by the faces and costumes than I am by the magnificent architecture. The Gallic and English faces, the Algerians, the blacks. Highland Park will really look stodgy after this ...

"... The hotel is charming and there's a darling little young concierge and what looked to me like a frightfully lumpy bed turned out to be the down comforter that has been keeping me cozy when I do hop in. *Mais il n'y avait pas du savon dans la chambre* (I told you so!).

"My God! It's two-thirty—and I want to get up at eight ... Goodnight ...

"P.S. I found a marvelous use for *le bidet.* I fill it with hot water and soak my feet in it to warm them before going to bed.

"P.P.S. Won't you change your mind? It isn't too late—if you *hurry! Spend all your kisses,* Mr. Smith."

I felt a strange surge of excitement as I read that final line, as if it had some effect on me that I didn't yet fully comprehend.

It was a phrase that had become something of a motto to us since that night, a year or two earlier, when I had come across it while reading by Coleman lantern in

Mexico. I had never heard the phrase before, and it struck me as remarkably good advice. I read it aloud to her, wanting to share my discovery, but though she appeared to be listening, looking up from her own book, I had no idea that she would ever think of it again.

In the book I was reading the line was ascribed to some Roman poet, or Greek, perhaps. I must remember it, I told myself, and search out the poem at the library in Los Angeles. Sometimes, when I come across something I want to remember, I mark the page or make a note on a slip of paper, but more often I foolishly persuade myself that I can remember it without props. Then in a day or two I not only can't remember the book, but can't remember the thing to be remembered itself, having only a vague idea that there was something I wanted to remember.

I remembered that quotation, and now and then I quoted it, or Denny did, when it seemed appropriate. But I soon forgot the name of the poet, and forgot what book I'd found it in. I looked in a dozen books, thinking it would turn up, but it never did. To this day I do not know the name of the poet, and I have never encountered anyone among my more erudite friends who knows it either.

And there it was before me again, a postscript to a letter. The phrase had many uses, we had discovered. It may have been purely a sensuous thought. Poets are not unknown to spend all their kisses. But surely it meant also that there is no point in taking any of one's riches into the next world. Why keep a kiss, a gesture, a word that might give a moment's pleasure or reassurance to someone else? Money you can't take with you. Kisses you can't leave behind.

I read the letter again and looked up a number in the phone book and dialed it, with a tremulous hand.

"Thank you for calling Air France," said a cool female voice. "Can I help you?"

"I want to fly to Paris," I said, "as soon as possible. To-day. One person. First-class."

It might be difficult, she said. There was a steward's strike, and the airline was on a limited schedule. Perhaps I could wait a day or two?

"It's an emergency," I said. "A wedding. My son is marrying a Frenchwoman. There is no time to lose. I'm the father of the bridegroom."

Whatever their frailties, the French understand love and ceremony.

She put me on a jet, nonstop for Paris.

CHAPTER FOUR

There was no one to meet me at Orly airport. No one knew I was coming. I had sent a letter to the Joyeux residence, where they were all to gather, but Denny had been somewhere in the Alps with Doug and Mademoiselle Joyeux, looking for her father's native village. The letter, I learned later, had been politely set aside, and waited unopened.

I had told them I would stay at Le Grand Hôtel, an elegant old palace near the Opéra. I took a taxi from the airport and spent a fitful night in my room. Global flights upset the human clockwork.

In the morning I bundled up and went out in the streets. My face turned numb. Paris was icy. I walked up the Boulevard des Capucines to a sidewalk café. It was glassed in for the winter.

I ordered coffee and croissants and took my time, like any Frenchman at his amenities, watching the shopgirls trotting off to their situations. They were armored against the cold in suedes and fake furs and shiny vinyl, like play soldiers in the opéra comique. Their cheeks were red and their legs flashed blue and pink through the slits in their flapping skirts.

I left the café and stepped into the quick parade. I felt an almost unbearable good humor. What a fine thing to be a member of this species, so chic and clever and vivid! The day was mine. Alone in Paris!

My eye caught a gaudy painted sign above a cinema that was showing *Bob & Carol & Ted & Alice.* It showed Bob & Carol & Ted & Alice, all in one bed . . . IMAGINEZ, it said, TOUTES LES POSSIBILITÉS!

Ah, Paris!

I walked till I came to the Arc de Triomphe and turned into the Avenue des Champs-Élysées and walked to the Place de la Concorde, vast and familiar under the towering pink obelisk from Luxor. Alas, the place was disfigured, like most of the urban world, by parked autos.

Still, history did not die. It was here, I remembered, that Marie Antoinette had placed her head on the block. I felt a need to share this grisly scrap of knowledge. I had an urge to grab the nearest Frenchman by the arm and tell him, "This is where Louis went to the guillotine, you know, and Antoinette!"

I walked on into the Tuileries Gardens. Its trees were sticks, its pools icy, its nudes cold. It was bleak and beautiful, quivering with the spring juices inside it, waiting to burst out.

I walked through the courtyards of the Louvre and took the Pont Neuf over the river to the Left Bank and walked in narrow streets to the Boulevard Saint-Germain. It began to rain. I ducked into a bar and ordered a café and drank it slowly, looking around at the other patrons.

Near the door a stocky man with a stiff gray beard and a face like pink granite was looking down through gold-rimmed spectacles at a paper on his table, working at it with a pencil in his rawboned hand. The likeness was startling. But the man was years dead!

As I left the café I gave him a closer look. It wasn't

Hemingway at all, of course, nor even his ghost. It was only some lesser exile, working the crossword puzzle in the Paris *Herald-Tribune*.

I took a taxi back to the hotel. The evening was ahead. Alone in Paris. *"Imaginez toutes les possibilités!"*

"Ah, Monsieur Smith," said the man at the desk. "A message for you."

It was a telegram from Tours. ARRIVING YOUR HOTEL ABOUT 8 P.M. PLEASE WAIT IN YOUR ROOM.

It was nearly ten when they came in; my wife and both our sons. They had arrived in Tours and opened my letter that day. Curt had got a pass and come over on the boat train from London, arriving just in time to join them. Mademoiselle Joyeux had stayed in Tours to prepare for the wedding. We walked to a café on the Boulevard des Italiens and had onion soup and mugs of Danish beer and were pleased with life.

In the morning my wife and our betrothed son set out to shop for a wedding ring and a pair of shoes. His old ones were down to the nails. I set out with Curt to see Paris. We were all to meet in the Louvre at noon.

Curt and I took the underground to Saint-Germain-des-Prés, on the Left Bank, and walked without plan in that exhilarating quarter, feasting on the scents of sausages and cheeses and the shop windows stuffed with the amenities of civilized life and the faces of people who seemed every one unique and valuable.

We paid three francs each to stand under the great dome of the Panthéon, not sure just which god we were to be in awe of, Yahweh or Bonaparte or Cybèle, and then walked a block to the Sorbonne, where students hurried down the sidewalks in their winter wraps, looking cold and hungry and exuberant, like extras in *La Bohème*.

We crossed the Seine to the Île de la Cité and entered Notre-Dame. It was cold. A mass was going on. Old men in red vestments sat in the choir stalls, singing the antique litany, their heads canted sideways on their necks, their faces old as stones.

We reached the Louvre on time. The others were late, and Curt suggested that we look into the hall of antiquity. We walked down an enormous corridor toward an atrium in which the Winged Victory of Samothrace soared headless against massive flights of stone stairs in a downpour of cloudy daylight. We climbed to another long hallway at the end of which the Venus de Milo waited for us in a vaulted chamber. We walked around her, seeing colors and scars and subtleties that a million copies had neglected.

Later, when the others came along, we lunched in the Louvre café on cold chicken and white wine. They had found a wedding ring in a shop on the Place de l'Opéra, but there had been some trouble about Doug's shoes. He had settled finally for a pair that were otherwise suitable, but squeaky.

"With every step," he said, "she's going to hate these shoes."

We started out in a little German Ford for Tours, escaping from the chaos of Paris traffic into the winter countryside. In midafternoon two spires appeared in the distance.

"Chartres," Doug said. "Isn't it fantastic!"

We drove into Chartres through medieval streets and parked below the cathedral and walked up to it and into the towering dim nave. We were alone, except for the ranks of stone angels and martyrs and one ancient woman lighting a candle before a patron saint.

It was tomb-cold. Only the candles and the light of the stained-glass windows gave any sense of warmth. It was utterly still. But I felt the presence of terrible and exalted spirits who had waited seven hundred years for this family of shivering Americans and an old woman lighting a candle.

It was dark when we reached Tours and crossed the river to Saint-Cyr-sur-Loire and drew up at the neat white plaster house on the Rue Foch where Mademoiselle Joyeux and her family awaited our arrival with a festive table.

"This is it," Doug said. He got out of the car and opened our door, and with every step his shoes squeaked.

My familiarity with Jacqueline's errant but engaging English had not prepared me for this first encounter with her parents. The Joyeux' lack of English was profound. Even Doug's prolonged visit had made no breach in that wall. Their English was no more abundant than my French, which is to say that between us there might have been a dozen words, in one language or the other, that were mutually understood, and these were soon battered beyond further service, like a shuttlecock in a doubles game between duffers.

My own ineptitude became apparent to me as soon as the door to the house was open and a small white feisty dog made for my ankles, yipping psychotically.

"Down," I muttered as he threw himself against my knees. He was not intimidated, however, and I realized with dismay that I didn't even know how to talk to a French *dog*.

"Clyde," scolded a girl who stood at the back of the crowd. She chastised the dog in his native tongue and he skulked away, biding his time.

Clyde? What a ridiculous name, I thought, for a dog.

But the warmth and hospitality of the Joyeux household soon transcended language. The house was two and a half stories high, but narrow, like a house in a medieval city. The lower floor was given over entirely to a dining room, which served also as the parlor, and a large kitchen. "My father," Jacqueline had told me, "he live to eat and drink."

Everything seemed almost clinically neat, but the table at the center of the stage was already set, dishes and flatware gleaming in the candlelight; and on a cabinet against the wall I saw a row of bottles, their contents ranging in color from palest yellow to deepest red. As my eyes fondled that lovely rainbow my tensions eased; here was the common language that Jacques Joyeux and I would share.

Maria Joyeux was as neat as her house, a well-kept woman, thin but well-shaped. Monsieur Joyeux was rounder than she, thanks, perhaps, to his love of food and wine, and bald as a monk. During the flurry of kissing and chattering that followed our entrance he said almost nothing, an activity in which I joined him, but our eyes met warmly. We knew we would find our meeting ground.

Monsieur Joyeux soon withdrew to the kitchen, our dinner being already on the stove. He was the village postman of Saint-Cyr, Jacqueline had told us, making his daily rounds on his bicycle; but he had once been a chef, and it was in the kitchen that he gave expression to the poet in the postman.

The girl who had rescued me from the dog soon sought me out. She was Jacqueline's younger sister, of course, Nanette.

"You speak French, yes?" she said in a burst of English which caused me to hope, for a moment, that we were about to engage in a long and enlightening conversation.

"No," I said. "But *you* speak English?"

"*Oui,*" she said. "I am study her at school."

We made faltering progress, mostly over the stepping-stones of her schoolbook English. I was soon enchanted. She was schoolgirl shy, but there was a boldness underneath, and wit, and she was vibrant with excitement over the visitors from America, the wedding, the sense of doors opening into a new world of unimaginable delights. She was a student at the Lycée Choiseul, which was in Tours beside the cathedral,

but she was eighteen years old, or near it, and soon she would
go to Paris to begin life.

Somehow the dog had got back in and was at me again.
I gave him a knee in the muzzle, hoping Nanette wouldn't
notice, and toppled him over, but he was up in an instant,
more furious than before.

"You do not like Clyde?" said Nanette, laughing at
me in her eyes.

"Clyde? Where did he get that name?"

"He is from your movie," she said. "I see *Bonnie and
Clyde,* I say, Clyde is good name for z'dog. Yes?"

Dinner began with onion soup. Monsieur Joyeux's pièce
de résistance was a dish made of Belgian endive, ham, and
Swiss cheese, and of course there was cheese and fruit and
a pastry. But my memory is mostly of the wines.

He had seized upon my appearance as a God-given
opportunity to demonstrate the wondrous variety and superior
quality of the wines of the Loire, and he intended that I
should not escape a single one. In this design, which both my
wife and his regarded as insidious, I was wholeheartedly
his accomplice.

My glass was never empty, except when my host emptied
the dregs of one wine only to speed me to the next. Glass for
glass we proceeded through his cellar, Monsieur Joyeux
naturally asking nothing of me in the way of capacity that
he was not quick to match himself. It became a ritual. The
wine poured, the glass raised, the bouquet inhaled, the mouth-
ful taken, the exclamation of approval; and all the while
Monsieur Joyeux's eyes anxiously on mine, watching for their
spontaneous tacit judgment.

For once in my life I was not unhappy to hear that there
would be no champagne with dessert; but this turned out to be
only because Monsieur Joyeux disdained champagne in favor
of the sparkling white wine of his own valley. It was indeed

a buoyant vintage, and it gave me the lift I needed, at last, to make it up the narrow wooden stairway to our bedroom on the top floor under the attic.

"Long live France," I sighed, and was soon as deep in slumber as all its kings.

I am an early riser, whatever my follies, and Jacques Joyeux evidently shared that virtue. When I went downstairs the next morning he was sitting at the table, drinking a milky-looking coffee from a cup the size of a cereal bowl. There was butter and jam on the table, and a great long loaf of bread. I guessed that he had already been out to the village bakery.

"*Bon jour,*" I said tentatively.

"*Bon jour,*" he said, not altering the tone.

We appeared to be the only members of the household who were up. He poured my coffee and we sat drinking and eating in silence, neither of us being noticeably well. Finally Madame Joyeux came down the stairs, then Nanette, then my wife, and one by one the others.

The wedding was not to be until the next day, and the drill for this morning, I was informed, was a visit to the nearby Château Langeais. Eager as I was to explore the medieval ornaments of the Loire, I had no stomach for a drive over icy roads that morning to tramp up and down stone stairways in an icy castle.

"I have a bit of jet lag," I explained.

But it was not thought proper for me to stay behind, and besides, we were first to take a taxicab into Tours, where I was to rent an automobile for the duration of our visit. The Joyeux had only their bicycles, and we would need a decent car for the wedding. As we left I envied Monsieur Joyeux, alone at his table with his third bowl of coffee.

We rented a fine new Renault sedan and drove over icy roads to the Château Langeais, a cheerless-looking stronghold built over the ruins of Fulk the Black of Anjou's keep, the oldest in France. It was tomb-cold, inside and out. A guide whose enthusiasm was no greater than mine led us from one cold chamber to another, wrapping us in shrouds of what he evidently thought was English.

Shivering and mildly vertiginous, I stood in the great chamber where Charles VIII had married Anne de Bretagne five hundred years before, and wondered that anyone could have fallen deep enough in love to get married in a castle without central heating.

It was extraordinary how quickly my spirits rose at lunch. Monsieur Joyeux had a repast waiting for us when we returned from the château, including, of course, the indispensable wine. Though I had misgivings about drinking any, I was reassured by the first taste; it warmed me to my toes. By the second glass I was euphoric.

Then midway through the meal something quite remarkable occurred. Monsieur Joyeux placed his knife and fork in his plate and sat still for a moment while his eyes seemed to cross slightly and his pinkish face went green. Up he got to his feet, without an *excusez-moi,* and hurried up the stairs.

"Your father is not well?" I asked my intended daughter-in-law.

"*Oui,* Mr. Smith," she said. "He is not well. Last night he 'ave *too* much wine."

"That is too bad," I said, trying not to sound triumphant.

CHAPTER FIVE

Our son and his betrothed were married on a snowy Saturday morning in the *mairie* (town hall) of Saint-Cyr, across the river from Tours.

They had considered marrying in the church, but the ecclesiastics of Tours were not propitiated by the bridegroom's credentials, or the lack thereof. I for one regarded this as a happy circumstance, suspecting that the town hall would be warmer than the church, and the civil ceremony briefer.

On the morning of the wedding the aunts, uncles, and cousins began gathering at the house on Rue Foch. There was an air of great excitement and much running up and down the stairs, and many bad jokes in two languages, and finally the bride descended in a full-length white satin fur-trimmed dress and white short jacket with fur-trimmed hood. Nanette, the bridesmaid, looked hardly less spectacular, and rather more worldly, in a chic black maxi coat and large-brimmed floppy hat. She carried a red purse and wore red mittens and a red band around her hat, and looked ready indeed to go to Paris and begin life.

We piled into four cars and drove through Saint-Cyr to the town square and parked directly in front of the *mairie,* the square looking as if it had been cleared of everything but a bicycle or two in expectation of our arrival. The *mairie* seemed larger than the Joyeux house. We climbed wooden stairs to the public meeting room where the ceremony was to be held. The room was spartan-plain, with rows of wooden chairs facing a long table.

A bust of La Belle France rested on a shelf above the table, and at the opposite end of the room, behind the chairs, a life-size bust of Anatole France stood on a pedestal with a plaque which noted that the illustrious writer had lived in Saint-Cyr, and at long last had wed his faithful housekeeper, Marie-Héloïse (called Emma), in this very room.

We settled into the chairs, and waited for the mayor to ascend the stairway for the ceremony. Two girls, the mayor's clerks, stood behind the table, turning the pages of a great register, and calling up the members of the wedding to sign in the proper places.

All was in order. We waited. Then we heard a measured step on the stairs. The mayor entered—a stately gray-haired woman in a beige and black dress with a silk sash—the tricolor of France—slanting down across her bosom.

Madame la maire walked with the dignity of Charles de Gaulle to her place at the center of the table and sat beneath the bust of La Belle France, symbol of la République. The resemblance was stunning. With her classic face, a face that might have been sculptured by Houdon, with the gray hair combed straight back from the noble forehead, *madame la maire* was La Belle herself, though half a century older.

She beckoned the betrothed to come forward. The bridegroom took two curiously awkward steps, almost as if he were limping. Was something wrong? An instant later I remembered. The shoes. He was walking in a special way to keep his new French shoes from squeaking.

The *maire* began to read, rapidly, in French, the words coming out fluent and musical, like a jazz solo on the clarinet. She asked her questions and received, apparently, the right responses. *Oui.* Yes. *Oui.* I understood little, but once I caught my son's name. It was a question, followed by a momentary silence. *La maire* looked up expectantly.

"*Écrivain,*" he said at last, as if having made an on-the-spot decision.

The *maire* finished. She beamed. She handed the bridegroom a parchment stamped with the seal of Saint-Cyr. The ceremony was over. Chairs scraped on the wooden floor. There was much handshaking and hugging and kissing and laughing.

"Did you hear that?" my wife said aside to me as we moved toward the stairway. "*Écrivain?* He gave his occupation as a writer."

A writer. So that was what the word meant. Well, I thought, why not? It was better than being unemployed.

As we passed by Anatole France I gave him a wink. For a young *écrivain,* it seemed to me, the mischievous old skeptic would make as good a patron saint as any other.

We all gathered for a moment on the steps of the *mairie,* the bride like an enchanted white rabbit in her fur-trimmed hood. The icy air rang with joyous shouts and laughter.

Then snow began to fall; very light and beautiful and ephemeral. The flakes were tiny and bright and fell slowly, melting in the street.

We all hurried to our cars and drove out in the Loire Valley to Vouvray, where the wines are made, and sat down to a wedding feast in a warm inn called Le Val Joli.

On such a morning it was understandable why the French had invented the phrase *la joie de vivre.* It was a morning for weeping with joy, and of course some tears were shed; but there was more laughter as we gathered around a long table at Le Val Joli. It was a hunting lodge, or had been one, and the walls were hung with paintings of huntsmen in the woods with their dogs.

I had hoped to sit next to Nanette, so I might continue her English lesson, but the unattached girls in the party moved automatically to the side of my older son, the young American airman with the guardsman mustache. He sat between Nanette and one of her pretty cousins, and I observed that he seemed to have no trouble amusing both, though his French was no better than mine.

I found myself between an uncle and an aunt, I believe they must have been, who spoke no English. But fortune did not ignore me altogether, for my friend Jacques Joyeux was seated on the far side of the aunt I had drawn, and he, of course, was in charge of the wine. In the exercise of this responsibility, he performed with nothing less than the vigilance and generosity I expected of him.

That I would be grateful for a sip or two of wine became apparent as soon as the food began to arrive. First, for the appetite, we received plates heaped with seashells, some of them looking quite paleolithic, from which we were expected, I gathered, to extract the viscous flesh with an assortment of tools that lay beside each plate like instruments set out on a dental surgeon's tray. One of them, which appeared to be a nutcracker, was to be used, I saw by watching the others, for cracking the more stubborn of the creatures that had been wrested from the sea for this occasion. *Fruits de mer,* these delicacies were called. It is a term I am not likely to forget.

I eat shellfish reluctantly, since I am not fond of them to begin with, and there is some evidence that they give me hives. Thus, I made a perfunctory pass at a clam or two, then washed them down with a white wine from one of the two bottles which, thanks to Monsieur Joyeux, stood within easy reach of my plate.

The *fruits de mer* merely made me feel uncomfortable. I was afraid I would be thought quite rude, neither speaking the language nor eating the food. By polite exclamations of appreciation for the wine, however, accompanied by histrionic smiles and gestures, I hoped to express my good intentions. Indeed, all went well enough until the next course came.

I suddenly found myself looking into a plate on which lay two dead birds. They were hardly larger than sparrows, and for all I knew *were* sparrows. They had of course been plucked, but the remarkable thing about them, to my mind, was that they still had their heads and their feet. I was undone. I find it hard enough to eat fowl in any form, without thinking of the whole bird, soaring from tree to tree in glorious life. Never had I been asked to put knife and fork to a bird that looked as if he might put on his coat at any moment and fly away.

Not only was I unable to eat my birds, I was unable to watch my companions eat *their* birds; and when I heard my new daughter-in-law utter a tiny cry of delight as hers were placed before her, I wondered if after all our son hadn't made a mistake; if there were not cultural barriers one ought not cross.

It was only a momentary defection, of course, and my spirits returned as soon as I poured a glass from the bottle I had not previously tried. A most remarkable wine, I thought. It seemed to go straight to the head, and by the time I had drunk half a glass my fears and inhibitions were so thoroughly repressed that I might have tried one of the birds, if I hadn't already sent them away.

I had no idea how rapidly I was being anesthetized, however, until I essayed a scrap of conversation with the aunt on my left while pouring myself another glass, only to see her point, in great agitation, toward the bottle. Not quite in time, I saw that I was missing the glass and pouring that remarkable vintage, whatever it was, on the tablecloth of Le Val Joli.

Afterwards we piled into the Renault and Doug drove us out to the Château Amboise, which is said to have been the first work of the French Renaissance in the valley of the Loire. In my judgment it was colder than the Château Langeais had been, if that was possible, and larger, and the English was no better. As I stood freezing on the balcony from which the Huguenots had been hanged, I groped for some profound observation on man's inhumanity to man, but all I could think of was the warmth of the Joyeux house, and the bed on the third floor under the attic. More than anything I wanted a nap.

At dinner that night I tried to find out from Jacques Joyeux, with Jacqueline interpreting, the name of the wine that had made such an impression on me at the inn. The question seemed to make him very merry.

"Mr. Smith," said Jacqueline, "my father say that z'bottle was not wine. It was *cognac*."

Everyone laughed, and Monsieur Joyeux raised his glass to me.

"He say," said my daughter-in-law, "you were *magnifique*."

CHAPTER SIX

On Sunday morning after the wedding, Denny and I took the train from Tours back to Paris and caught an Alitalia jet for Rome.

"It will be warmer in Italy," I promised her.

It was a short and beautiful flight over the snowy Alps, with a lunch of sausages, smoked salmon, cheese, and beer. The stewardess who brought it looked strikingly familiar.

Lollobrigida? No. Podesta? Not quite. Her face was younger but older; young but ancient. It was the face of a minor Venus I had seen in the Louvre; the same Augustan brow, the same sculptured nose; the same small voluptuous mouth and dimpled chin.

It is historically improbable, I have read, that any citizen of modern Rome is directly descended from the ancient Romans; the old blood is gone. But this girl's face denied it. She was surely the daughter of some goddess who rose three thousand years ago from the Ionian Sea.

She came down the aisle again, pushing a cart loaded with green and amber bottles.

"*Birra?*" she asked me.

"*Oui, oui,*" I said, with more enthusiasm than was seemly. We were in Italy now, I reminded myself. I would have to forget my French.

It was too cold in Rome to wait for a bus. We took a taxi.

"Hotel Texas," I told the driver. He nodded and we leaped away in his Fiat.

"My Italian must be pretty good," I told Denny. "At least I can say Texas."

The streets of Rome were rivers of tiny demented cars, racing to their doom like lemmings. Every traveler tells of this phenomenon, but it is not easy to describe. Only a Dante could portray such chaos. Rome has fallen; not to the barbarian this time, but to the automobile.

The *pensione* Texas occupied the two top floors of a sixteenth-century palazzo on the Via Firenze. Like most of Rome's structures, it had been renovated inside, but the Renaissance facade, patriotically protected by law, remained intact. The Texas had been recommended to us by a friend. "Don't let the name fool you," he said. "It isn't anything like Texas."

We ascended to the fifth floor in an iron cage. The office was an antique desk and chair in a foyer. The lobby was a Renaissance salon, no larger than our living room at home.

"I am Mario," said the man at the desk. He showed us to our room. It also had a touch of elegance, though it was less opulent than the lobby. A window looked into the street and across to the other facades, all of the same style and ocher color as our own. I felt as if we had been locked up for the night in a museum.

Later we had an apéritif in the salon with the proprietor, an urbane Florentine named Agnolucci. Signore Agnolucci told us the building had once been the palazzo of a count who died in disgrace.

"He betrayed Italy?" I asked.

Signore Agnolucci sighed. "Exactly! He was responsible for the monument to Vittorio Emanuele. As you will see tomorrow, it is an abomination!"

I thought of the abominations in our own Civic Center, back in Los Angeles. The men responsible never died in disgrace though; they were re-elected.

Our first morning in Rome we had breakfast in our room. The main reason for traveling in Europe is to have breakfast in your room. The fare never varied. Rolls and butter and jam with strong coffee and hot milk. I had not eaten jam since I was a small boy. After one week in Europe I was going for seconds. It seemed quite civilized. I would never eat bacon and eggs again.

It was cold in Rome. I put on a sweater and over it my fleece-lined corduroy coat and over that my fleece-lined raincoat.

When we stepped out into the Via Firenze there was a light rain. We dashed to the corner and took shelter in a coffee bar.

"Where do you want to go?" I asked.

She dug in her purse. Someone had given her the address of a glove shop on the Via Barberini. I dug out my guidebook and unfolded the map of Rome.

"No problem," I said. "We're quite close."

We set out for the Via Barberini. The cold was invigorating. We walked fast. The blocks of ocher palazzos and gray churches flew past. We soon learned how to get across a street with our lives, eluding Fiats like matadors eluding bulls.

It rained again. We ducked into a shop and bought an umbrella for two thousand lire. I also bought a jaunty plaid rain hat. At the next corner I unfolded my map and studied it again.

"It's down this street," I said, and we set off at an angle down a brick alley, jumping puddles and flattening ourselves against the buildings to escape mayhem or death from cars and motor scooters.

We came to a street down which, half a mile away, I saw the ancient gaping walls of the Colosseum. It is a sight that has the force of thunder.

"Ah, Rome!" I exclaimed. "You set out to find a glove shop and you find the Colosseum."

We walked down the street to the Colosseum and entered it through one of the great arched gates and climbed to the stone tiers from which the citizens of Rome had looked down upon their bloody games. What a tub of awful memories it was!

From the Colosseum we looked out over the Roman Forum, and beyond and above it, rising over the noble ruins like a wedding cake in flight, we saw the massive monument to Victor Emmanuel II, white as false teeth. I realized why Signore Agnolucci had told us the count who designed this extravagance had died disgraced.

We climbed to the Palatine Hill, where the emperors built their palaces, trampled mud in the house of Augustus, and walked in the ancient Forum among the tumbled marbles. I found the ruins of the rostrum and climbed to a spot from which, I fancied, Mark Antony had harangued the populace over Caesar's body.

"Say something!" Denny shouted. "I'll get a picture."

"Friends, Romans, countrymen," I began, but it was no use. My lips and tongue were too cold for classic oratory. Caesar's ides must have been in a warmer March.

I raised my hat and aimed my umbrella at the mob.

"Who do I look like?" I shouted.

"Rex Harrison!" she shouted back.

That evening we had an apéritif with Signore Agnolucci in the Renaissance salon of our pensione and asked him how to find the Via Barberini.

"You will have no trouble," he assured us. "It is quite close."

Rome was colder than Paris. In the morning I looked out our window into the Via Firenze. It was wet.

"Let's go down to Naples," I said. "We can take the train."

"I'd like to find that glove shop first. My hands are frozen."

"Don't worry. It will be warm in Naples. Ah, sunny Napoli!"

We packed one bag and caught a taxi to the station. A train was departing for Naples at the hour. We bought second-class tickets. First-class was for snobs.

For fourteen hundred lire we bought a lunch to take on the train in a paper sack—a huge ham sandwich, a chicken breast, a handful of olives, a piece of cheese, and a small bottle of red wine.

We shared a compartment with two Italian men. They ignored us. We watched the walls and aqueducts of Rome slide by us and then the beautiful Italian campagna, strewn with the rubble of centuries. The Apennines were white.

The train arrived at Naples on time. We stepped down to the platform with our suitcase and our lunch. It was raining. A man in a blue uniform headed toward us like a bird dog. A badge on his cap said TRAVEL AGENT.

He led us through the station and across a frenzied piazza to a warm little office where he stretched out a map of the Bay of Naples. He laid out our plan.

We would be driven, in a private car, to Pompeii, and then on to Sorrento, where we would have a room for the night, and dinner. In the morning we would take the boat to Capri, for lunch, and then sail back across the bay to Napoli. All for thirty-two thousand lire.

On his map the bay was azure, the isle of Capri a warm beige. I looked out at the rain. "We have no choice," I said.

Our driver was a battered little man; a vanquished

bantamweight. He was an expert with his Fiat. We stopped on the road for a lunch of the local fish and wine, then sped on to Pompeii.

He waited in the car while we walked under our umbrella over the ancient stone paths among the fallen villas. Vesuvius, which had buried the little town, stood white in the dark sky. It looked benign.

My spirits rose as we flew over the road toward Sorrento, a place whose very name filled me with nostalgia, though I had never been there. The Bay of Naples was gray and rumpled. The sky was pewter. The driver pointed to Capri. It was on the gray side of beige.

"The wind blows in from the sea," he said. "Tomorrow is sunshine. You will see."

He delivered us to our hotel. It was one of a long strand of small new hotels in Sorrento, strung out along the seaport like a miniature Miami Beach. The rain had stopped.

"Is too cold for rain," he assured us.

Before dinner we walked to the town piazza, with its heroic statues and old church and shops and cobbled alleys, and its faded luxury hotels, closed for the winter, clinging to the sheer cliffs above the tiny port. We looked down, far below us, and saw the creamy white island boat, bobbing at its pier like a toy in a blue plastic tub. This was the boat that tomorrow would take us to Capri.

We hurried back to the hotel for the dinner arranged for us by the man in the blue cap. The dining room was a sea of white tablecloths. There was only one other couple. They were Italian. It was quiet. The windows overlooking the Bay of Naples were dark. A waiter in a starched white jacket made us an apéritif at the little bar. The Italian couple kept their voices low; so did we.

In a while another guest came down; a woman, alone.

She was in her forties, plump and plain, but somehow attractive. She had perhaps been very pretty. She took a table for two and ordered an apéritif and sipped at it, looking about with a desolate smile.

I fell into my Somerset Maugham routine: She was obviously English . . . Her husband, a tobacconist, had recently been the victim of a dreadful but clever murder . . . She had been tried and acquitted, and had come to Sorrento to forget, or more likely to meet her lover-accomplice . . .

"She looks like a dear little thing," Denny whispered.

"You never can tell," I said.

Suddenly the quiet was torn by an insane shouting. A television set was glowing above the bar. The reason was soon plain. There was an international soccer match on the tube —the British Celtics against the Florentines. The waiter sank hypnotically into a chair, his eyes on the screen. It was a noisy match, announced in passionate Italian. After what seemed hours the Celtics scored a goal, and then another. Gloom clouded the face of the waiter.

The English murderess was also watching, or pretending to. The English middle class had little else to do, I imagined, but watch soccer on TV. The match ended. The British had won. The Italian couple left. I ordered a liqueur. The waiter was sullen. The Englishwoman looked over at us, offering a timid smile.

"I'm going to ask her over," I whispered. "I don't care what she's done."

"How very kind of you," the Englishwoman said, settling down at our table. She ordered a whisky and Coke.

Yes, she had recently been widowed. Her husband was a shipping agent in Brighton. He had been cut down untimely by a stroke. Their children had insisted she go away for a holiday in southern Italy.

"I'm so lonely, luv," she said. "I'd go home tomorrow. But of course I can't let the children know. They think I'm having a beautiful time."

Sometime during the night the storm broke. We were startled full awake in our beds by a terrible clap of thunder.

"What was it!" Denny shouted, sitting up. "Vesuvius?"

There was a white flash. Then more thunder. Rain lashed at the window. I looked out. The Bay of Naples was in agony.

I got up and opened the quarter-bottle of wine that had come in the sack lunch we had bought at the station in Rome. It turned out to be an unassuming little *rosato,* but it cheered us up.

In the morning the bay was too rough for the boat to Capri. We packed to go back to Rome. I left five hundred lire for the chambermaid, and the sack lunch as well, along with the empty bottle.

On our last day in Rome we set out to find the little glove shop.

"I'd like to get my hands warm just once," she said.

The shop was on the Via Barberini, only two blocks from our *pensione.* Fumbling at my map of Rome in the cold, though, I must have got it upside down. We took the wrong direction and came to a river.

"It's the Tiber," I said. "Think of the history these old shores have seen!"

We walked along the Tiber, past the Castel Sant'Angelo, whose dungeon had once held Benvenuto Cellini, and came to St. Peter's. It has never been my favorite church. It is too vast. Standing in its nave is like standing in the Grand Canyon. I don't like to feel that small. But the great Bernini colonnades reach out and draw you in like pincers. We entered and were engulfed. We found Michelangelo's Pieta, back in its chapel after a perilous voyage to America. It occurred to me that I rather preferred the marble copy back home in the Hollywood Wax Museum. Was the light better there? I put the thought out of mind. It was sacrilege.

You could spend a lifetime in St. Peter's, studying its treasures, as you could spend a lifetime in the New York Public Library reading books. But I prefer the streets of Rome to its churches. The streets of Rome celebrate life. Besides, there was the glove shop to be found.

If that happy word "serendipity" had never been coined it would have to be coined for Rome. Our search for a glove shop had already taken us to the Colosseum and the Forum and St. Peter's, and then, that last day, we stumbled into the piazza of the Trevi Fountain.

First we heard the sound of rushing water. Our steps quickened. We turned a corner and there it was, that marvelous hunk of exuberance, the Trevi, with its athletic gods and mighty thrashing horses, struggling to escape their eternal stone.

I thumbed to the Trevi Fountain in my guidebook: "The origin of the legend, according to which all those who throw a coin into the fountain must return to Rome, is lost in the darkness of the ages."

We walked on, our spirits high.

"You didn't throw a coin in," she said.

"No. It's too cold to come back."

It is a short walk from the Trevi Fountain to the Piazza Barberini, which is where the Via Barberini begins, but we turned into the Via Sistina to look for the Spanish Steps.

It was snowing lightly when we came to the top of the steps. We walked slowly down, under our umbrella, like Lunt and Fontanne descending a staircase in some cosmic production of *Idiot's Delight*.

We took cover in a small café on the Piazza de Spagna and had a lunch of artichoke hearts, antipasta mista, and lasagna, with a bottle of Lacrima Cristi.

My serendipity was all used up for the day. We found the glove shop at last, but it was closed. All the shops in Rome are closed in the afternoon from one to four, for wine and pasta and, so they say, making love.

We walked on in the cold. I carried the umbrella so my wife could keep her hands in her pockets.

From Rome we flew back to Paris for one last day. It was a Sunday, a day so cold and so beautiful that we ached from the cold and the beauty of it.

We had a room in a small hotel on the Left Bank, four flights up and no elevator, around a corner from the Place Saint-Germain-des-Prés, with its old cafés and old church, the oldest church in Paris.

Church bells woke us, the sound deep and measured; old bells, the same bells that had awakened Molière and Berlioz and Alice B. Toklas, and might at this very moment be waking a new Voltaire.

We walked down the Boulevard Saint-Germain to the Seine, and then across the bridge to Notre-Dame. A priest in red, the archbishop himself perhaps, was singing the mass in French.

We walked down the south aisle and stood in the light of the great rose window, beside the statue of St. Joan of Arc. The maid seemed supple and alive in the light of half a dozen votive candles.

The priest's voice was high and reedy against the deep distant voice of the great organ. Then he called the communicants to the altar and they streamed forward to receive the bread and wine.

The organ music soared. It grew wild and awful, like

some cosmic river flooding. It filled the church. The very stones seemed made of sound. It burst into an exaltation that was almost unbearable, and then the power drained away and left only a plaintive aftersound, a few notes tumbling after each other in some playful fugue.

I was trembling, but not from the cold, as we walked out into the daylight.

"You seemed quite shaken back there," Denny said after a while, "for an unbeliever."

"Yes," I admitted. "But I'm not an unbeliever. I believe in Bach."

We had lunch in a glassed-in sidewalk café on the Avenue des Champs-Élysées, warming ourselves first with a *lait Gabrielle,* a nectar made of hot milk, honey, rum, and cinnamon.

The Sunday promenade was in full tide. Tens of thousands of Parisians were out on their splendid boulevard—the rich and the bohemian and the bourgeois; young lovers and old roués and married couples en famille, pushing red-cheeked infants in perambulators.

Up one side they came and down the other, walking swiftly in the cold, thick as crowds leaving the Rose Bowl after the New Year's game. The women were a carnival in their festive clothes; short skirts and long skirts and furs from chimeras and unicorns and other imaginary beasts.

If this was all that civilization had brought us to, a *lait Gabrielle* in a sidewalk café on a cold Sunday in Paris, watching the people walk on the Champs-Élysées, it had all been worth it, all the centuries.

We descended into the underground and took a Métro back to the Place Saint-Germain-des-Prés, and when we came up to the street again it was snowing.

We had dinner in an old restaurant from La Belle Époque, looking unabashedly at all the people and being looked at, sharing the communal sense of joy and excitement, and feeling quite lucky to be human.

The best part of any trip is the memory of it. Cold can not be remembered, and minor disasters become diversions.

We flew home from Paris nonstop, and when I stepped out of the plane to the ramp I was kissed by a breath of warm air off the Pacific.

It was so pleasant, so reassuring, that I felt as if the world had never been any other temperature. It had been like this in Rome and Paris. My memories of Rome and Paris would always be clothed in the warm wrap of Southern California weather.

I had parked my car at the airport. We took the San Diego Freeway and then turned east over the Santa Monica. It was dusk, a time of day in which Los Angeles is at its best, smog or no smog. In the last hour of daylight the view from the Santa Monica Freeway is beautiful. That is a word not often spent on Los Angeles. We are Double Dubuque. Smogville. The Nowhere City. But if beautiful sounds extravagant, consider the extravagance of the view:

To the north the Hollywood Hills and the Santa Monica Mountains, a backdrop that would surely have pleased Cézanne. To the south the peninsula, dark in the sea; and beyond it—on a clear day—Catalina, which from a distance at least, is quite as pretty as Capri. And easier, I had found, to reach.

What nature has provided, man has enhanced. The towers of commerce, so easily despised, are works of art from the changing perspective of the freeway. In the darkening sky they give more light than the Pyramids. They celebrate neither the past nor the hereafter, but the present.

The automobile has created Los Angeles. It is destroying Paris. The Place de la Concorde is a parking lot; the Avenue des Champs-Élysées a logjam of tiny beeping insects. No one knows how to drive. The taxi drivers are insane.

Our Santa Monica Freeway was made for the facts of this century. It allows us to see what we are like, at fifty-five miles an hour. No other avenue in the world moves one so fast through such a spectacle.

And when you get there, I am asked, where are you?

Well, you are in a city that knows what century it is living in. You are in a city whose Water and Power Building, when lighted from within at night, is more striking than the Panthéon.

And anyway, whether you believe all this or not—you are home.

We were glad to be home.

CHAPTER SEVEN

It was a poignant April. First Curt came home from England and we went out to UCLA together for the annual Mardi Gras. He was due to leave the Air Force in the fall, and he wanted to go back to the university and get his degree. Like many of his generation, he had enlisted to resolve the uncertainty of the war and the draft. The beautiful Westwood campus, now tranquil after the turbulent '60s, stood for everything he had left behind, and everything he hoped to come home to.

The Mardi Gras was held on the green field between the new dormitories and the old brick halls on the hills above the sunny splash of Janss Steps. We bought a string of tickets and tried a few rides and games of skill. It was early in the day and the other revelers were mostly children.

The booths were tended by UCLA girls; more cooks in every kitchen than were needed. They turned out to be the part of the Mardi Gras my son liked best. I was standing in line for a hot dog on a stick when I realized I had lost him. I walked back and found him looking at an ice cream booth.

SOPHOMORE SWEETHEART ICE CREAM, the sign said.

"You want some ice cream?" I asked.

"No. See that girl in the booth?"

She had Lady Godiva hair and a beach-girl figure and was wearing a demure white apron.

"Watch," he said.

She turned around and reached into the freezer to scoop up some ice cream. Under the apron she wore a little black mini. He sighed. So did I.

"All the time I was in England," he said, "it was winter."

We walked on.

"Step right up," a young man barked over a mike. "Win a Frisbee!"

For one ticket you got three chances to throw a Frisbee through a hole in a canvas wall. If one went through, you won a Frisbee. I got in line. Two small boys in front of me won Frisbees. My turn came.

"Sorry, sir," said the girl in the booth. "I'll have to charge you two tickets. You're—uh—not that young."

I thought she had handled it with tact. She might easily have said I was too old. I didn't win a Frisbee anyway.

We had pizza pie and teriyaki on a stick and then Curt said he was still hungry.

"You feel like an ice cream sundae?" he said.

We walked back to the Sophomore Sweetheart and ordered two chocolate sundaes.

"It's been four years," he said, watching the girl scoop up the ice cream. "I wasn't sure they still looked that good."

I could have told him he needn't have worried. They would always look that good.

Then Doug and Jacqueline came back from France. He found a job working nights, and for a few weeks, while they were house-hunting, they stayed with us.

It was a good chance for me to get better acquainted with Mademoiselle Joyeux, for I still thought of her as that. We weren't yet easy with each other. She still called me Mr.

Smith, and though I called her Jacqueline, and grew more enchanted by her every day, there seemed to be a vague tension between us; a distance that neither knew how to cross. I imagined that she still saw in me the personification of everything difficult about America.

Like many Frenchwomen, she had developed a supple wit to protect her from male autocracy in a male chauvinist world, and often enough I felt its quick, light touch. She was elusive, though, and given to swift attacks followed at once by that disarming innocence. I was never sure whether to say "Touché" or "Sorry."

When she was home with us those evenings we tended to rely on television for entertainment. It eased the conversational strain, and at the same time gave our daughter-in-law a rather intensive course in American manners and morals. There is no better way to absorb our idiom and our attitudes than by watching old movies. They were the mirror in which we saw ourselves the way we wanted to be.

One night we were watching a movie from the 1950s and I realized how far we had come since then in dealing with sex on the screen. I am not necessarily in favor of complete candor, but those old movies might have been easier to follow if the sexual encounters had been a little more explicit.

When movies were censored we never knew for sure whether anything had *happened* or not. There were clues—that look in Katharine Hepburn's eyes in *The African Queen;* lines like, "Please, Roger, don't spoil everything"; and music, always music, building up big and powerful and cascading over us in the fadeout.

I knew, and you knew, perhaps, that something had happened; that the plot had taken a critical turn, that it would never be quite the same with Clark and Ava again. But those scenes often went over the heads of innocents who didn't know life, or had just moved up from Hopalong Cassidy.

In one of the movies we saw on the television en famille, Richard Burton was a doctor who fell in love with Barbara Rush, the wife of Burton's best friend, Larry, who was dying of Hodgkin's disease.

Ordinarily I wouldn't have watched it. I'd had it with movies about doctors' dilemmas. But our daughter-in-law liked soap operas because everybody talked slow and said everything twice. "My God, Fred, I've suffered! How I've suffered! But I love you! I love you!" That made it easier for her to understand.

Everybody in the movie felt guilty. Burton felt guilty because as a boy he had seen his mother in bed with the gasman, Jimmy Dunn, and blabbed it to his father, who took it so hard he jumped to his death from a Cape Cod cliff. You didn't see all this, though. Burton told it in a choked-up monologue against a pounding surf of background music.

"Mr. Smith," said Jacqueline, "I do not understand. What does he say?"

"He said his father killed himself because his mother was unfaithful," I said.

"Really? For *zat* he kill himself?"

"This is Boston, Massachusetts," I pointed out, "not France."

Later it happened. Barbara Rush followed Burton down to his boat and he tried to comfort her over Larry being in such bad shape. They were standing on the deck in the daylight. He took her in his arms and the music rose and there was a fadeout to a Sleep-Eze commercial.

In the commercial a man couldn't sleep so his wife gave him a Sleep-Eze and he had a good night's sleep. "Tonight," the announcer said, "why don't you slip someone you love a Sleep-Eze? You'll both feel better in the morning."

Jacqueline left the room during the commercial and didn't get back until after a scene in which Barbara Rush told Burton she was going away to New Haven to have her baby.

"What 'appen?" she asked.

"Barbara Rush is going to have a baby," I told her.

"She is *enceinte?*"

"She is what?"

"*Enceinte.*"

"Oh. *Enceinte,*" I said, trying to copy her pronunciation. I hadn't come across that word but once or twice since high-school days, when I was devouring the works of Guy de Maupassant. The French always had a better word for any-thing to do with women. *Enceinte* sounded so much more elegant than "pregnant."

"*Oui,*" I said. "She is *enceinte.*"

"Zen zey mus' have gone farzer zan I s'ought," she said. "I s'ought he only kees her."

"You could tell by the music," I explained.

She wasn't convinced. "Zere was a bed on z'boat?"

I hadn't thought of that. There could have been, though. It looked like about a twenty-five-foot sloop; it might have slept two. I'm sure you can see that a brief, explicit sex scene, nothing in bad taste, would have saved me a lot of trouble.

Finally Burton told Larry about the baby. Larry cringed. "Don't suffer!" Burton pleaded. "Please don't suffer! Nobody should ever suffer!" Then he slipped Larry a fatal dose of morphine and Larry went to sleep. It made me think of the commercial.

"Now they'll both feel better in the morning," I said.

"Ah, Mr. Smith," she said, "you 'ave no heart."

"I could hardly keep from laughing," my wife told me later that night, "when Jacqueline wanted to know if what's-her-name was *enceinte*."

"Why is that?"

"Because *she* is, you know."

"She is what?"

"*Enceinte*."

"Who is?"

"Your daughter-in-law, of course."

I guess the grandfather is always the last to know.

Not long after that revelation, with its implications of my own changing status, I had yet another one to ponder.

We have always had a few heirlooms: a porcelain clock with gilded angels on it; a chamber pot now planted with some kind of succulents; a set of pewter—all kitsch but very precious. These things come down from some romantic past, beyond memory, where heirlooms are supposed to come from.

But it gives a man a start when he finds that something he bought in his youth is regarded already as a family heirloom. When one buys something new he does not expect it to become an heirloom in his own lifetime. The things we buy new *stay* new, don't they? Like the faces of friends we see every day, they never change.

True, my younger son has an easy chair that belonged to my father. My father left it to me, and I used it for years and then passed it on to Doug when he was married. So the chair is already in the third generation. It's as sturdy as ever and sound enough for a fourth generation, I'm sure. Then it will be an heirloom. I don't think you can call something an heirloom until it has seen four generations.

What worries me is the mirror.

I bought the mirror for my mother on her birthday, as I

remember, a year or so after World War II. It was a large, oblong mirror to be hung on a wall. My mother hung it in her living room to give an illusion of space, a decorating trick that was then in vogue.

In time the mirror came down to Denny and me and we hung it in our living room to give an illusion of space. The mirror-space-illusion vogue had passed out in favor of Van Gogh prints, but we needed all the space and illusion we could get.

Later, when our sons grew tall enough to see over the top of a dresser, and vain enough to comb their hair, we put up a Van Gogh print where the mirror was and hung the mirror in their bedroom. There it had remained through the vicissitudes of recent years.

For a long time I hadn't given the mirror a thought. Now that my wife used the extra bedroom for sewing, she was the only one who frequently saw the mirror. I don't know whether she ever looked into it or not.

Then one day we were getting ready to visit Doug and Jacqueline in their new house. It was Jacqueline's birthday. There was a large, flat package against the wall. Denny was writing on a card.

"What are we giving her?" I asked.

"A mirror. You think that's all right?"

"Mirror?"

"Yes. All she has is a hand mirror. She needs a larger one."

She did indeed. She was expecting, and a young woman in that state ought to have a decent mirror, to watch the progress of her miracle.

"Do you mind putting it in the car?" Denny asked.

It seemed remarkably heavy.

"Where'd you get it?" I asked. "It weighs a ton."

"Where'd I get it? Why, out of the bedroom. It's ours. Didn't you know?"

Jacqueline was delighted. I saw at once how impossible it would have been for her without a mirror. She was before all else a daughter of France, and I could not imagine a Frenchwoman without one.

I sat in my father's easy chair watching her as she got acquainted with the mirror, regarding it first with apprehension, then with curiosity, then with a certain smile. Today, perhaps, the mirror was not at its best. Time would change that.

It struck me. Soon enough another person would look into that mirror, perhaps experiencing the same emotions, from fear to self-approval.

She would be—good Lord—my granddaughter! She would be the fourth generation to see herself in that mirror, that heirloom.

I got up out of my father's chair and looked at my mother's mirror. It had turned gray, I noticed, at the temples.

CHAPTER EIGHT

Newcomers spending their first year in Southern California like to complain that they miss the seasons.

"The trouble is," you'll hear them say, usually when you're all sitting around the pool, "you don't have any seasons out here."

Actually, we have very nice seasons. It's just that when we get up in the morning we never know what season that particular day is going to be.

It occurred to me one afternoon that it was fall. I was sitting in my rocking chair in the living room listening to a Mendelssohn concerto on the phonograph. The sun was low and the light coming in from the patio was yellow. It seemed alive and touchable.

I knew that if I wanted to see what fall was like I'd better go out and look, before dark. In the morning it might be spring.

Working in the city and running down to our house in Baja on weekends, we had been neglecting our yard. The gardener had come round for an hour or two on Tuesdays and kept it alive, like a doctor making a perfunctory house call; but it looked unloved.

I put on my corduroy jacket and went out to walk my acre, feeling like a landed squire. I let the poodles out of their keep. A gentleman walking his land in the autumn likes to have a dog or two at his heel. They went mad, dashing about and filling the air with mindless yipping.

None of our pets had ever turned out intelligent—had never, in fact, matured. The poodles were getting along, but their behavior was infantile. They were nothing but overbred lapdogs, after all. Someday I would get myself a man's dog.

With a stab of guilt I realized that it had been months since I'd really walked in the yard to look at things up close. The pink hibiscus was in flower, but there were as many blossoms on the ground as in the tree. I couldn't remember noticing when it bloomed.

The Chinese elm was brown and bare, its leaves scattered like old coins on the grass. They crunched pleasantly under my shoes, a sure sign of fall, even in Los Angeles. The Bermuda grass was brown.

The pepper tree had fought its annual struggle to the death with the passion vine, and won again. Its leaves flashed yellow in the wind like little knives around the lifeless dark carcass of the vine still coiled about its trunk.

I climbed the sturdy concrete steps I had built at such a great expenditure of brain and brawn. They were my Pyramids. Despite their mass they had a lightness, an illusion of flight, like the Spanish Steps of Rome. Perhaps I had missed my calling. I might have designed great monuments.

The fountain was dry. The naked nymph stood patiently in the dry bowl among dead leaves, holding up her platter, from which no water fell. I sat on the white cast-iron garden bench and looked at her—really looked at her, for the first time in months. That's all they ask, you know, that you really see them.

She would be called kitsch by some—a voluptuous female cast in concrete from some familiar but not quite faithful mold. Kitsch, perhaps, but our sons had given her to us for Christmas one year when they were schoolboys and I loved her as much as I could have loved an original Bernini. In the lemon sunlight of this autumn afternoon, here at the furthest reach of Western culture, she was a lovely nymph, an Aphrodite, a Rachel, a symbol of womankind before the liberation.

A red bauble caught my eye, then another. There were a dozen of them, red lopsided balls, in a bushy tree. Pomegranates. I picked a fruit the size of a baseball and took it inside. Pomegranates have always seemed unreal to me, a fancy of childhood, a mythical fruit, the food of unicorns. I cut it in half, exposing the tough yellow pockets full of tiny pink translucent pips. The juice squirted when I picked a cluster out, staining my fingers. I popped it into my mouth. It was both sweet and bitter, a taste like a memory of childhood.

If autumn was here, could spring be far behind?

There are certain momentous events in a family's history at which the presence of the patriarch is not only unnecessary, but sometimes a nuisance.

I had been planning to go see the Rams play that weekend, but it was possible that in my absence I might become a grandfather.

"Why don't you just go ahead," Denny said. "It's no great problem. There wouldn't be anything you could do, anyway."

Of course she was right. I had been at sea, somewhere between Iwo Jima and Maui, when I became a father, and I did not get home to see our first son until he was nine months old. It was unlikely that I would be needed for the successful delivery of a grandchild.

"Nothing's going to happen this soon, anyway," she said.

"All the same," I said, "maybe it would be better if I just stood by."

She left for Jacqueline's house and I took off my shoes and sat in my rocking chair, looking out the window into a darkening sky. It was beautiful football weather.

I wondered how long I would have to wait. I got up and put on a Glenn Miller record and opened a beer. I turned the phonograph down low, so that the sound was more like an echo from the past, and found a dogeared Ross Macdonald mystery I had already read twice. There was no harm in nostalgia; not if you didn't try to live in it, but only used it to remind yourself that you had a past as well as a present; and a future.

But this time it didn't work. I couldn't get into the past. The present wouldn't let me go. I checked my watch. I gave the telephone ten minutes to ring.

I changed into slacks and an old tweed jacket and left a note: "Gone to the game after all. Don't worry. Love."

I found my field glasses and drove down to the freeway, wondering what it was I had meant her not to worry about.

I thought back to the war, when I was in the Pacific and Denny was expecting. She had taken advantage of my absence by vetoing my choice for a name, if our first child happened to be a boy. In the last letter I had written her before I was swallowed up in a landing, and we lost contact, I had suggested that we call him Lucky Jordan, after the hero of a recent motion picture starring Alan Ladd. Many weeks went by before our transport put my regiment back on Maui, and I found, among the dozens of letters in my mail-call packet, one that told me I had a son named Curtis Bresson Smith, the Bresson being his mother's maiden name. Actually, I liked it, though I realized it was two-thirds French. It seemed to me a good idea for all children, male and female, to preserve their mother's family name.

I knew my wishes would carry even less weight in the naming of my grandchild. Still, a grandfather has a right to make suggestions, and I had proposed Michele or Gabriele, for a girl, and Jacques for a boy, with Joyeux to be given as the middle name in either case. Jacques Joyeux Smith. It seemed to me to have a lot of class: and of course it would be an honor to both grandfathers.

It was a big game and I had to park more than a mile away from the Coliseum, but I didn't mind. Good football weather is good walking weather, and I was glad for the exercise, hurrying along the sidewalk with a stream of others going the same way, feeling an unspoken camaraderie. People were closing in from all directions, swarming over the surrounding park toward the stadium.

I found a ticket booth and stood in line. I would be lucky to get a ticket at all and had no hope of getting a good one. It didn't matter. Just being there was the important thing. If we were going to keep football alive we had to sell the seats in the end zone as well as those on the fifty-yard line.

"How many in your party?" the man in the window asked.

"One. I'm alone."

"I've got a single for seven dollars. It's the best seat left in the house."

"Where is it?"

"Right on the goal line. Ten rows up."

I bought the ticket and filed through a turnstile and bought a hot dog and a sack of peanuts and a program and found my seat. I was alone in a sea of empty yellow seats, but they soon began to fill. Even then I felt alone, isolated among noisy cliques and amorous couples.

It was all right, though, once the Rams took the field. A man can identify with his team. They were Arthurian knights; they wore my colors; they shouldered my cause. In my eyes they were chaste—a flight of 250-pound angels.

There were seventy thousand of us there. At half-time

I swept my glasses around the stadium, looking into a vast motley wall of wraps and faces. I lowered the glasses and swam back to the tiny island of my own identity.

It was a good game; not a great game. I don't remember what the score was, or even who won, but I do remember that when I got home the house was empty. I phoned Doug's house but no one answered. I tried reading. I watched a movie on TV. The phone rang. It was Denny.

"I tried calling you earlier," she said. "Everything's fine. It happened sooner than anyone expected. You're a grandfather."

"It's a girl?"

"It's a boy."

"Jacques Joyeux?"

"No . . . Christophe Pierre."

"You mean Christopher?" I said hopefully.

"No. Christophe. It's French."

So there was no granddaughter yet to inherit the mirror. But maybe Christophe Pierre would like football in a few years, and I would finally have a relative who understood me.

It wasn't until a day or two later, when they got the birth certificate, that we found out it was really spelled Cristophe —without the *h*.

Jacqueline explained: "I am still dope up from my shot when this lady come to say, 'What is the baby's name?' and I forget how to spell Christophe. Now it is too late."

It didn't matter much to me. I planned to call him Pete.

CHAPTER NINE

One art form I had long since grown beyond, I hoped, was the horror movie, but I found myself watching them again, though not by choice.

Horror movies were Jacqueline's favorite TV fare. Her English still wasn't quick enough to pick up all the thrusts and parries of fast dialogue, and in that regard horror movies are even better than the soap operas. They have very little dialogue at all, and it runs to freak and creature talk, which is quite slow; or to Fay Wray screams and hoarse cries of "My God, Dr. Peabody, it's come back!"

Our son was working until midnight, and Jacqueline often came to our place evenings with her infant to watch horror movies on TV until time to pick him up. She would not only watch the early ones, but also the late ones, which didn't begin until eleven o'clock. This was both a blessing and a curse.

By midnight, when she had to leave, the movie was only two-thirds over. Then she begged me to watch the last third, after she had gone, so she could phone the next morning and find out how it ended. Of course I hadn't seen the first two-thirds. I'd been shut up in my den, trying to read. When she left, and I took over, I never had the murkiest idea what was going on. In the last third the story always degenerated into an orgy of screaming and bloodletting and then it was The End.

The next morning she would phone.

"Ah, Mr. Smith! You see z'end?"

"Yes."

"What happen?"

"I don't know. It was horrible. There was this dreadful fight."

"Zey kill z'monster?"

"I'm not sure. Which one was z'monster?"

None of these conversations ever ended in a satisfactory way, for either of us.

On Monday nights, though, it was even more frustrating for us both, because of the conflict created by the regular Monday-night pro football game on the tube.

I couldn't always get home for the kickoff at six-thirty. So I would phone home and if Jacqueline was there I would ask her to turn the game on and watch it for me. I knew she wouldn't watch it. She understood football even less than my wife did. But she would turn it on for me. That kept her from turning on the early horror movie and being halfway through it when I got home. I wouldn't have had the heart to turn it off.

One Monday night I got home at half-time when the Browns were playing the Oilers.

"Who's ahead?" I asked. "What's the score?"

"I do not know who is the teams."

"The Browns are in white and the Oilers in blue."

"Zey all look purple."

She was right. She hadn't adjusted the color. It was hideous. The Oilers looked like eggplants.

Then she and my wife went shopping and left me alone with the baby. I had never been alone with him before.

"What'll I do," I asked, "if he starts to cry?"

"He will not cry."

As soon as the sound of the car died out, he started to cry. I couldn't even hear the quarterbacks calling signals. I put him in the bedroom. He cried louder. I picked him up and took him back to my chair and held him so he could see the screen, and rather to my surprise he stopped crying.

He was still watching the game when they came back. His mother beamed.

"Ah, you hold z'kid!" she exclaimed.

"Z'kid's going to be all right," I said. "He likes football." She swept him up, away from such depravity.

There weren't any horror movies that night, but later I found them watching *Toys in the Attic,* that humid Deep South tale of murder and decadent love. Worse than horror. They were all watching it. My wife, my daughter-in-law, and my grandson.

I could see a battle shaping up for the kid's mind; or was it for my own?

In April our daughter-in-law's sister, Nanette, arrived from France to spend the summer. She had captivated me the night I met the Joyeux family in Tours, and I was delighted that I would be seeing her again. It was her first visit to America, and I was eager to introduce her to our culture in Los Angeles, so she could go back to France and tell them Paris wasn't the only city of light in the world.

I thought I might especially be able to help her with her English, while she helped me with my French. Though both my daughter-in-law and my wife spoke French, neither of them had ever seemed to have much enthusiasm for speaking it with me.

The very first time we had Nanette and Jacqueline over for dinner, though, I saw that French would have to be excluded at family gatherings or Mademoiselle Joyeux would never learn a word of English, and I would never have the slightest idea what was being said. I felt like a foreigner in my own house. It was like being in Paris in a hotel room and turning on TV and watching a panel discussion among three women, all chattering in that nasal Gallic tongue.

Finally I tapped my plate with a fork and said, "From now on, ladies, English *only* will be spoken at the dinner table."

I didn't wish to be autocratic, but merely to provide an environment in which the young lady might learn to speak pure English, as it was spoken by a man who was born right here in Long Beach. They all fell silent.

"Would you like some cauliflower, Nanette?" I asked.

"Eh?" she said.

"Cauliflower," I said, lifting the dish.

"*Ah, oui,*" she exclaimed. "*Chou-fleur.*"

"Cauliflower," I repeated. It means colored flower."

"It may mean colored flower in English," my wife said, "but in French it's *chou-fleur,* and it means *cabbage* flower."

"Eh?" said Nanette.

"Never mind, *ma chérie,*" I said. "Eat your cauliflower. It's good for you."

I didn't push the lessons any further at that meal, and the next evening I volunteered to take them all out to dinner. We went to a Bob's Big Boy in Santa Monica. I thought it would be a nice ride over the Santa Monica Freeway. We all had Big Boy hamburgers and ice cream sundaes.

"Sunday?" said Nanette. "It is *dimanche?*"

"Not Sunday," I said. "It's *sundae.* S-u-n-d-a-e. It means ice cream with syrup on it."

"Sur-rup?"

"He means *sirop,*" my wife said. "He always calls it surrup."

The Americanization of Mademoiselle Joyeux was proceeding very well. I was a born teacher. She had already mastered cauliflower and sundae and would soon enough be handling surrup like me and John Wayne.

On our first outing together I took her to the zoo. Given a language gap and a generation gap, it seemed to me that a zoo might be a good meeting ground. A zoo is a kind of United Nations. To the animals, French and English must seem quite the same. Animals remind us of the oneness of man. When you look into the eyes of an orangutan, you see neither Frenchman nor American, nor even the savage man of Borneo. You see us all.

"What would you like to see most?" I asked once we were inside the gate.

"You have snakes?"

I saw that Mademoiselle Joyeux might turn out to be difficult, like her sister. "Yes," I said, without enthusiasm. "You like snakes?"

"Oh, no. I am afraid. But I like to *see* them. Yes?"

We walked entirely around the snake house, examining every exhibit. It seemed miles. My span of attention for snakes is very short. I know they are remarkable creatures, perfectly adapted to their function, which is to eat other animals alive. But I hope for more than that, even in reptiles.

Somewhere near the snake house, as we left it, I pointed out a weeping willow tree beside a lagoon full of swans and cranes.

"That's a weeping willow," I said. "Isn't it pretty?"

"*Comment?*"

"Weeping willow. It's called weeping because it looks sad. The branches are bent over and the leaves seem to be falling, like tears. You see?"

"Ah, yes. We have this tree in France. She is called *saule pleureur*."

"What is it you say?"

She spelled it for me. "It is the tree who cries."

It was a good beginning. We had exchanged two of the loveliest phrases in one another's language. She had learned weeping willow, and I had learned the tree who cries.

I hoped to show my protégée the real Los Angeles beneath the pleasure-park artificiality of Disneyland, Knott's Berry Farm, Busch Gardens, Magic Mountain, and the zoo. So one morning I picked them all up—Mademoiselle Joyeux, Jacqueline, and the kid, and drove them down to Ports of Call. Nanette would be able to go back to Paris and say she had seen a New England whaling village in San Pedro, California.

With two naive Frenchwomen and an infant in my charge I felt a responsibility to be instructive. But I had learned already that somehow, in that company, I usually wound up feeling more ignorant than before.

We were no sooner parked and out on the wharf than we came to one of those stands where you pay a girl to dive for an oyster in a pool, and if there's a pearl inside, the pearl belongs to you. The two young women discussed it in French.

"Mr. Smith," my daughter-in-law said, "she doesn't want to try it."

"Why not?" I asked, wondering if she was always going to call me Mr. Smith.

"I think zey put z'pearl in z'oyster," said Nanette. "It is not really *belong to* z'oyster. No?"

"No," I said firmly. "I mean *yes.* It belongs to the oyster. Is that what they teach you in France? That Americans are dishonest?"

"No, zey do not say Americans are dishonest. But Americans do funny things. Yes?"

"Yes," I said, feeling lucky to get out of it that cheap, "we do funny things."

We climbed to the top of an old river steamer for a fish

lunch from the snack bar and sat at a table by the rail, looking down at the harbor channel. A passenger freighter moved by us on her way out to sea, flying the flag of the American President Lines. PRESIDENT POLK was lettered on her bow.

"That's the *President Polk*," I told Nanette. "You know who he was?"

"No," she said, looking at me expectantly.

"I don't either," I said, "for sure."

Cristophe tossed a french fry overboard to a squadron of sea gulls. It was thirty feet to the water, and I was keeping an eye on him.

"Mr. Smith," his mother said, "what would you do if z'kid fall in? You would dove in to save him?"

"Dive in," I said automatically, wondering why she always called him the kid. It was just some Gallic perversity, I supposed. "No, I wouldn't dive in. It would break my neck. I'd jump in." And almost certainly drown, I realized gloomily. I hoped I wouldn't be tested. I had got through life so far without having to be a hero, and I didn't want to be one now.

We strolled through the village to the fishpond and walked up on the foot bridge. Large red koi carps were foraging in the murky water, smooth and quick as sharks. A man in rubber knee boots waded out and reached into the water to work on a pipe.

"It is not so profound," said Nanette.

"What is not so profound?" I asked, wondering if I had missed some thread of the conversation.

"Z'water," she said.

"Oh. Profound. In America," I explained, "we say the water is *deep*. We say profound for a deep idea, in the head." I pointed to my head.

"*Oui*," she said, pointing to her temple. "We say *profound* also for z'head."

It was one of our more profitable days. Mademoiselle Joyeux learned that we Americans do not put artificial pearls in our oysters, my daughter-in-law learned that I would risk my life, if need be, to save her child, and all of us learned the meanings of profound.

CHAPTER TEN

We thought we had our transportation problem fairly well in hand when my wife bought a used Cougar and gave her old red Mustang to Curt and I took back my old Dodge convertible, which I had given him when he got out of the Air Force, and gave my Renault to Jacqueline. I thought having a little French car might make her happier.

The harmony achieved by these adjustments prevailed slightly more than twenty-four hours. The next night I was at work in my den, bogged down on a project that had to be finished by morning. The phone rang. It was Jacqueline.

"*Allo,* Mr. Smith," she said. "It's me. Your daughter-in-law."

"Yes," I said. "I know."

She was out for a ride in the Renault with her child and her sister and the Renault had broken down. It had simply quit. There was no juice. It was dead. She could not call her husband because he was at work. The car was at Sunset and Alvarado.

"We are in front of the little Mexican café," she said.

I knew that if I got in the old Dodge and went to her assistance I was in for a bad night. Few of life's ordinary contingencies can wreck a day more thoroughly than a car that breaks down. There is a negative dynamism in these situations. They always get worse. Every step one takes turns out, in retrospect, to have been an error.

"Wait there," I said.

I drove out in the Dodge. There was a Mexican café on the northwest corner but I didn't see the Renault. Then I saw it, catercorner across the street in front of a car wash. The car wash had a little taco stand. It must have been the taco stand that she called a Mexican café.

They were sitting in the car. I lifted the hood and looked into the engine. "I can't see what's wrong," I said.

"My father," said Mademoiselle Joyeux, "he would kick z'car."

"I thought your father didn't have a car."

"Yes. He 'ave no car. But he kick his bicycle when she is not work."

I crossed the street to a gas station to call the auto club. The dispatcher asked where the car was parked.

"It's in front of a Mexican food stand," I said, wondering if I shouldn't have said car wash.

It was forty-five minutes before the truck came. It rolled up in front of the Mexican café across the street. The driver looked around, said something into his radio, and seemed about to leave. I ran across the street, shouting.

"They told me a Mexican café," he said.

"I said a Mexican taco stand," I said. "This is a café. That's a taco stand across the street."

"That's a car wash."

We were both in low spirits when he pulled up behind the Renault. We got it started with a charge from the truck. I gave my daughter-in-law the key to the Dodge. "Go home," I told her. "I'll drive this one."

I was halfway home when the lights went out and the car died. It was a corner with a Thrifty drugstore, a Safeway supermarket, a Shell station, a dime store, and a Jack-in-the-

Box hamburger stand. If I was stranded, it was at the very crossroads of western civilization.

I called Doug from a phone booth at the gas station. He would come after me, but not until he got off, at midnight. "I'll wait here," I told him.

At midnight the gas station closed. Nothing was open but the Jack-in-the-Box, a bar next door, and an all-night mortuary down the block. I sat on the curb and surveyed my surroundings. It occurred to me that the Jack-in-the-Box was a good piece of pop design; functional and amusing. It was doing a good business for that hour, too. The mortuary was also lighted up, but it wasn't doing any visible business; just waiting, trying to look like a plantation house in the antebellum South.

I went over to the Jack-in-the-Box for a cup of coffee and sat at an outdoor table, analyzing my situation. I should have stayed home and sent my wife for my daughter-in-law. I should have had the Renault towed to a garage and driven everyone home in the Dodge. I should have phoned my wife to come after me instead of my son. I was alone on a street-corner in the middle of the night. There was nothing to do but wait. Doug arrived at twelve-twenty-five.

"I guess you've had a bad night," he said.

"Not that bad," I said. "It was better than being dead."

I'd rather spend an hour in a Jack-in-the-Box, any time, than in a mortuary.

I decided to phone Dr. Reap at home one morning. I rather dreaded doing it. Dr. Reap doesn't like to be phoned at home by his patients, even those who happen to be his friends as well. He puts in a lot of hours at the office and the hospital and he considers his home his castle.

Naturally I had phoned his office first and got his assistant, Miss Winter. "He's staying home this morning," she told me, "because of the fire."

I looked out the window. Dr. Reap lives at the top of our hill and lives, as we do, with the possibility of brush fires, especially in the fall after a dry summer and before the first rains. If he had a fire up there I would have been able to see the smoke. The sky was clear. Reap was probably staying home to play with his Rolls-Royces. He collects Rolls-Royces the way I collect sports coats.

"There's no fire that I can see," I told her.

"Well, he's worried that there might be. He's taking precautions."

That sounded like Reap. He's an activist, always at the barricades; usually, though, he merely dictates a letter into a machine on his desk at the office. I don't know if he actually mails any. I think he just keeps the tapes and plays them back to himself and some of his patients, if they happen to be Democrats.

Once when I had a suspicious liver he played me a letter he had dashed off to John Foster Dulles. Now that I think back on it, I had no idea it was that long ago that he first began to watch my liver. I don't think he ever mailed that letter. In any case, Dulles never got it; at least he never acted as if he had.

"It's sort of an emergency," I told Miss Winter. "I have this inflamed gum, up around my second molar."

"Shouldn't you see a dentist?"

What I needed, I told her, was a periodontist, but my periodontist had died. I had of course phoned my regular dentist, hoping he would recommend a periodontist, but his answering service had never called back.

My periodontist, in fact, was not alone in having left me. I had recently lost an osteopath, which is bad news indeed for a man with a slipped disc. I've heard it said that men first begin to realize their youth is over when policemen begin to look like college boys. That's true. But there's a much more alarming sign, and that's when a man's doctors begin to die.

We live in an age of medical specialization. A man is no longer expected to squirm through life's narrows with only a dentist and a family doctor at his side. By the time he is middle-aged he will have put together a group of specialists; a team; a phalanx of experts on each of the misfortunes to which flesh is prone.

Thus, I had once been in the care of, or at the mercy of, as the case might be, not only my late osteopath, but also an ophthalmologist, a periodontist, and a urologist, not to mention Dr. Reap—a formidable group to which I had most recently added a promising young dermatologist.

Of that original group, only the urologist, the dermatologist, and Dr. Reap were left, and two of them were my seniors. Dr. Reap had been with me more than twenty years, and while he had yet to diagnose me in any satisfactory way, he had become something of a crony—a literate, compassionate, and charming man, if somewhat testy. It is my view that friendship is better for you than a diagnosis.

It seems ironic now that it was my late ophthalmologist who introduced me to the realities of my own deterioration.

"You know, Mr. Smith," he said to me during my first refraction, "after we pass forty—uh—our muscles aren't as —uh—strong as they used to be."

"What are you driving at?" I asked.

"I'm afraid," he said, "we're going to have to have bi-focals."

So it was logically to Dr. Reap that I turned, then, when my group began to fall apart. He and the young dermatologist were the nucleus around which I hoped to build a new team. I was in much the position of George Allen when he went to Washington to rebuild the Redskins. Unlike Allen, though, I had no desire to trust my fortunes to men who were already over the hill.

"Well," said Miss Winter, "if it's that kind of an emergency, you might as well go ahead and call him at home."

I dialed his number. I imagined he would be close to the phone, ready to call the fire department the instant he smelled smoke. One ring. Two rings. Three.

I was inclined to hang up. Either he wasn't there, in which case I might as well hang up, or he was having to come a long way to get to the phone, and would certainly be out of sorts.

Five rings. I had decided to hang up when he answered. He sounded gruff and out of breath, like a man who has just surfaced after struggling for his life with a man-eating octopus in sixty feet of water. I thought of hanging up without saying anything, but I dislike people who do that.

"Did I get you away from something?" I said at last.

"I was up on the roof."

It was worse than I could have imagined. "Oh," I said. "Up on the roof?"

"I'm putting in a sprinkling system. What's your crisis?"

"What I wanted," I said, "is to ask if you could recommend a good periodontist."

"I don't even know what one is," he said.

"Mine died," I said.

"What about your regular dentist? Is he dead too?"

"I don't know," I said. "He may be. He isn't answering his phone. My eye doctor died too, you know, and my back doctor." I was hoping to stir some professional sympathy.

He was silent. It must have struck him just as it had me
—he was the only man left on my team. We were survivors.
There were somber implications in that for both of us.

"Well," I said, "sorry I bothered you. Get back on the
roof, and for God's sake be careful!"

"No problem," he said, almost gently. "You better come
in for a checkup. You hear me?"

I finally got through to my regular dentist. He wasn't
dead after all. He sent me to a periodontist; a young man—in
his middle thirties, I would have said—and apparently in
good shape.

"I'm glad you turned out to be so young," I said. I told
him the story of my thinning team.

"Don't worry," he said with a reassuring smile. "I'll
outlive you."

That was an encouraging prediction, but a moment later
he gave me the bad news. He had been scrutinizing my X rays
and found something he didn't like at all.

"I'm afraid you've got a molar here," he said, "that will
have to come out."

"You want to do it now?"

"Oh, I don't do extractions," he said. "Don't you have
an oral surgeon?"

I was back where I'd started. My team was one man
short.

CHAPTER ELEVEN

Most men have had the experience of watching a game with a woman who really isn't interested. It can be exasperating, but also amusing. Generally, it makes a man feel superior.

It is more exasperating than amusing, though, to watch a game with a wife, a daughter-in-law, and the daughter-in-law's sister, when none of them really is interested and two of them speak more French than English.

When the Los Angeles Lakers played the Milwaukee Bucks in their playoff opener, I would have gone to the game, rather than watch it on TV, but unfortunately it was being played in Milwaukee. Jacqueline and Nanette and the baby had come over for dinner, but Doug was still on the night shift and had gone to work.

When the game started, the women were all cooking dinner: a meatloaf. I was glad to have them in the kitchen instead of the living room, though I don't know why it would take three women, two of them French, to cook one American meatloaf.

The game was close. Everyone had expected Los Angeles to die quickly, and for a while it looked as if they would. Twice they fell behind seven points in the first half, but die they didn't. They hung in there.

Wilt Chamberlain was fantastic. He played under the basket like a seven-foot Nureyev. "Did you see that!" I shouted when the Stilt leaped up to block a shot by the great Alcindor. I was shouting in the wilderness. There wasn't even an echo.

I had expected to watch only the first half, by which time the Bucks would have the game on ice. But at half-time the Lakers were leading by a point. It was incredible. I got up and turned the sound down to quiet my nerves.

"It is over?" my daughter-in-law asked.

"No. It's just the half."

"Who's ahead?" my wife asked.

"We are. It's forty-four to forty-three."

"Who are we playing?"

It's when they try to be polite that it's hardest to bear. When the third quarter started Jacqueline came out of the kitchen and sat beside me on the sofa.

"For which color do you cheer?" she asked.

"Purple. We're the purple ones."

"Purple? What is purple?"

"It looks brown," I said. "It's the TV. It's supposed to be purple but it looks brown. My God—did you see that!"

Mademoiselle Joyeux came out of the kitchen and sat beside her sister. "It is football?" she asked.

"Basketball," I said, making the motion of shooting a basket. "Bas-ket-ball."

Her eyes lit up. "Ah, *oui*—basketball!" she said, adding something enthusiastically in French.

"What?" I said.

My daughter-in-law translated. "My sister says that in France she has play basketball many times."

"Ah, *oui*," I said, wondering what kind of basketball young ladies must play in a French provincial high school.

"Dinner's on the table," my wife said.

"I'm not eating," I told her. The Lakers had gone ahead five points and I had really begun to believe they might do it. My stomach was a lump.

"It'll get cold."

"Let it get cold. I can't eat."

I don't know whether the meatloaf got cold or not. I never did eat. But the Lakers certainly got cold. They went absolutely scoreless for four minutes, while the Bucks were scoring thirteen points. When the horn blew at the end of the third quarter, though, they were only six behind. They could still pull it out.

"It is over?" said my daughter-in-law.

It was over, all right. I just didn't know it. The last quarter was a slaughter. The Bucks outscored us by fifteen points and won the game by twenty-one.

I turned the TV off. The three of them were watching me from the dinner table. In the candlelight their eyes were full of mockery. Somehow it made me think of the opening scene of *Macbeth,* where the three witches are stirring up their pot of trouble. The way the Lakers had played, it had to be witchcraft.

But Nanette and Jacqueline were affectionate and respectful again on Father's Day, though I would just as soon have been left alone.

For years I have tried to phase out Father's Day. I consider it silly and commercial. If a man had the respect and affection of his wife and children, he would have it every day. If not, there was no use in setting aside one day of the year for perfunctory demonstrations.

But it isn't easy for a father to phase out Father's Day. The more he protests that he doesn't wish to be the object of any extraordinary attentions, the more he is suspected of inviting them. A man who is truly modest and self-effacing is rarely taken seriously.

So I thought of getting at Father's Day through Mother's Day, which fortunately comes first. I simply phased out Mother's Day. It seemed to me that if I gave up Mother's Day, the other members of the family would sooner or later get the idea and give up Father's Day. It's oblique, but I've discovered that in some families the oblique approach is best.

So I ignored Mother's Day completely, except to give my wife a jar of sweet pickles. Of course that was only a joke. I happen to love sweet pickles in liverwurst sandwiches, but she rarely remembers to keep them in good supply.

I also gave her the annual explanation of my attitude. It was just that I resented being obliged by some nationwide sales pitch to express, through merchandise, an essentially private sentiment engendered by years of proximity and interdependence.

"I know," she said.

I realized I had won her over when she decided to leave me on Father's Day and drive down to our house in Mexico alone. It was a symbolic act of liberation for us both. I could spend the day in solitude, reading and reflecting. Father's Day should be a day for introspection, for adding up one's wins and losses and striking one's balance.

I was carrying out this plan when the phone rang. It was Jacqueline.

"It is you Mr. Smith? You are at home?"

"Yes, of course. I am at home."

"Good. We will see you later."

A few minutes later Curt phoned. "Are you going to be home?" he asked. "I thought I might drop by."

Curt was back in UCLA, determined to finish the education his time in the Air Force had interrupted, and was working on the side as well, so we hadn't been seeing as much of him as we would have liked.

He arrived in an hour with a young woman I hadn't seen before. She had dark hair and dark eyes and a sunniness that made me think of Italy.

"This is Gail Paolucci," Curt said.

They were the Paoluccis of San Fernando Valley now, but they had come from southern Italy a generation or two ago, by way of Buffalo. She looked thoroughly American, this Miss Paolucci, but I had an idea she could put together a proper lasagna. She was taking physical therapy at UCLA, and they had met in chemistry. Evidently some chemistry was already at work. I was reminded of the day Doug had first come up the hill on his motorcycle with Mademoiselle Joyeux.

Curt and Miss Paolucci had brought me a large plastic bag full of water, with a rather fancy goldfish in it.

"For Father's Day," he said.

I had been phasing out my goldfish, much in the way Denny had been phasing out my pickles, by neglecting to replace them as one by one they disappeared. But this was a pretty fish; maybe just what I needed to restore my old enthusiasm.

Soon Doug arrived with Jacqueline, Cristophe, and Nanette. Nanette was carrying an enormous black puppy with a white spot on his chest.

"Not for me!" I said weakly, trying not to show my dismay.

"He is partly a Labrador retriever," said Jacqueline.

"A retriever?" I said, wanting to say that the last thing in the world I needed was a retriever.

"And part Dalmatian," said Nanette.

"Z'white spot," said Jacqueline, "zat is z'Dalmatian part."

"His name is Stepan," Doug said.

"Stepan?" It was all beginning to seem surreal, like a scene in a bad French movie.

"He's named after Stepan Bandera. You know, the Ukrainian rebel."

My familiarity with Russian history did not encompass Ukrainian rebels.

"He rebelled against the Soviet Union."

Much to my relief it turned out that Stepan Bandera was theirs. They had brought me something else. My daughter-in-law carried the gift into the house in a bulky sack. I viewed it with apprehension, but I knew it couldn't be worse than a dog.

"So you will not give them any more to your wife," she said.

It was three quart jars of pickles. I was touched.

So it turned out to be a rewarding Father's Day after all. I was so relieved not to be getting the Labrador retriever that I drove all six of them down to Venice for a festive Greek dinner at the Cheese and the Olive.

"How do you think the Rams will do this year?" Miss Paolucci asked me as I sipped a glass of retsina.

"Better than last year, I hope," I said.

"I'm afraid they have a quarterback problem," she said.

I was astounded. Here was a young woman who not only knew how to cook lasagna, unless I was mistaken, but also understood football well enough to know that the Rams had a quarterback problem. Miss Paolucci, I decided, was a treasure.

I soon grew fond of the goldfish. He would always remind me that he might have been a dog. And I had enough sweet pickles to last me to the next Father's Day, which I hoped to spend alone in quiet introspection.

The best thing about Father's Day, though, is that pre-season football is only a month away. It might seem that I would have given up trying to interest Jacqueline and her sister in American sports, considering their failure to respond to a simple and exciting game like basketball. But we sports fans are evangelical at heart.

I have never even been able to explain my feeling for football to my wife; I don't know what made me think I could explain it to foreigners, especially women. The French are atrocious at games. They are even worse than the Italians, who are only slightly better than the Greeks. Neither the French nor the Italians can beat the English or the Americans at any game but political intrigue and sex, which the French, especially the women, have always regarded as inseparable.

I tried to explain that to Jacqueline and Nanette the night I took them to the exhibition game between the Rams and the Cowboys at the Coliseum. Nanette had never seen sixty thousand people at one time before, it being impossible to get sixty thousand Frenchmen together for anything less than the defense or overthrow of Paris.

All the way to the Coliseum I was in high spirits: airborne with anticipation. The season, so long awaited, was here. It would go on and on; a feast. Not until mid-January would it come to an end in the most awesome civil contest man had yet conceived—the Super Bowl.

The Rams ran out on the field in their white jerseys and then the Cowboys in blue, and I explained to Nanette which was which.

"You are for the whites?" she asked.

"Yes. They're Los Angeles. They're the Rams. The ones in blue are from Texas. They're the Cowboys."

"They are cowboys?"

"No. They're professional football players, but they're called cowboys because they're from Texas. It's symbolic."

When the Cowboys scored the first touchdown Nanette clapped her hands. I was embarrassed to find myself annoyed.

"Why are you cheering for *them?*" I asked.

"Everybody else cheer for the whites. I cheer for the blues."

"Well, you wouldn't," I said, "if you'd ever been in Texas."

It was in the third quarter that the peanut man came up our aisle. He was an artist. He had more poise and control than anyone I'd seen since Sandy Koufax. He could throw a bag of peanuts thirty feet, right into the cupped hands of the customer. For variety he threw from behind his back or between his legs, hardly ever missing, and when he did miss, small matter; the bag was caught by someone else and hustled on to its destination.

Getting the money back from the customer was more chancy, but the peanut man made some fine catches, and when he missed a coin the fans were happy to look for it at their feet among the paper cups and hot dog wrappers. One coin sailed over him and fell in the row just ahead of us. For the next two minutes six people tried to find it for him, but finally the peanut man released them from the search. "Don't look for it any more, folks," he said. "It's part of the game."

During the ten minutes in which he worked our neighborhood, engaging the undivided attention of Mademoiselle Joyeux, there was an interception, a brilliant kick return, and a touchdown.

By half-time, though, I had explained the function of the pass, the punt, and the yellow handkerchief, which she liked the best; and the blues were leading by two touchdowns.

There was a half-time show on a stage under the peristyle, the theme being "It's a Small World." There were gaudy tributes to Mexico, Japan, and France, which were represented by their traditional ethnic dances, the French dance being, of course, the can-can, and then a tribute to the United States in which the band played "God Bless America." Old Glory lit up in the sky in fireworks, a giant Statue of Liberty blazed on above the peristyle, rockets burst in the night, the announcer shouted "It's great to be an American!" the crowd sang "God Bless America" and the band played "The Stars and Stripes Forever" as the blues and the whites streamed out for the second half.

"I think you Americans," said Nanette, "are very chauvinist."

"If you think *that* was chauvinism," I told her, "you should see a half-time show in *Texas*."

There had been one enchanting moment in the show, though. Remarking that the astronauts of Apollo 15 were at that very moment descending from the bright American moon that hung above the peristyle, the announcer asked every person in the crowd, at the count of three, to light a match as a salute to those three heroic men. The lights were dimmed, the count came over the speaker—one, two, three— and in an instant, all over the Coliseum, tens of thousands of flames appeared and the crowd uttered a deep, tremulous, spontaneous sigh.

Beside me Nanette cried out with joy and clapped her hands. For her, it was the high point of the evening. It was mine, too, except for that big pass the whites completed in the first quarter, Gabriel to Snow, sixty-seven yards for a touchdown. God bless the Los Angeles Rams.

"Do you realize," I asked Nanette on the way to the car, "that you have probably been watching the best football team in the world?"

"Zey have football teams in other countries?"

"Well, no. Only Canada. But what I mean is, if there *were* football teams in other countries, the Rams would still be the best in the world. Nobody can play football like Americans."

"Ah, *oui*," she agreed.

The next morning Jacqueline phoned to thank me for taking her sister to the game. "She really had a good time," she said.

"Good. I was afraid she wouldn't understand it."

"Are you kidding, Mr. Smith? She *love* the fireworks and the peanut man, and when everybody lights up their matches in the dark."

It was a beginning. If I could get her to another game or two she might actually understand the draw play.

CHAPTER TWELVE

Everyone seems to be searching for old values and old standards of excellence these days, and we found them one evening that summer at the Hollywood Bowl.

We shared a box with friends named Torgerson, and shared also a picnic feast of marinated roast beef, fruit salad, and garlic bread. Denny had prepared the basket and Torgerson brought a bottle of red wine.

We arrived as the sun was falling behind the hill, leaving a soft blue sky over the bowl with a light curtain of see-through cirrus clouds. The concert was two hours away, but the picnickers were already settling in with their baskets and bottles and Thermos jugs and cocktail shakers. Some set up tables and lighted candles.

Twilight came, that best part of the day, the hour that few urban Americans ever see any more, unless they are late getting home over the freeways and it falls on them. It is the hour now of the cocktail lounge and the TV set, the juke box, and the six o'clock news.

In the twilight the crowd was gathering. People rarely seem as beautiful as they do in that hour at the bowl; physically beautiful, in their casual clothes, as well as gentle and urbane and lucky. Wherever they come from, whether they sit in the boxes or the highest row, they are a true elite. Here is our species at its finest, brought together to hear Mozart and Bach and Beethoven under the stars. For the moment, it does not seem possible that elsewhere the world is turbulent and afraid.

The sky dimmed gradually, and it would seem to lose light quite suddenly, as if someone had pulled a switch backstage. Then a minute later whoever was doing this pulled another switch and the cirrus clouds turned pink.

Two or three stars came on, as if programmed. The bowl was filling. Here and there a wine or martini glass would catch the pink light. It was one vast festive picnic, but quiet; only a soft fountain of voices, with spurts of laughter.

"The moon will be up," I said, having looked it up in the paper.

"How do you know?"

"One knows."

It rose, waxing, only two nights from full, the moon on which our astronauts had so recently walked. It would never be possible to look at the full moon again without thinking of machines and men.

Someone pulled another switch and it was dark except for the moon and a few stars and the glow of the shell. The maestro marched out to the podium with the bearing of a sergeant-major taking over a battalion on parade. Applause. He bowed. He turned to his orchestra.

The silence seemed perfect; all sound was enclosed in a tremulous soap bubble. It is a thrill, that silence, that splendid discipline of twenty thousand people, stilled by the promise of beauty, imminent and immense.

The baton was up. The maestro made his move and then came the long, rich opening sound of the *Egmont Overture,* like an announcement: "It is I, Beethoven. I am here."

"I wish," I said when the overture ended, "that Beethoven *could* be here."

"Yes," said Torgerson, "instead of standing downtown in Pershing Square with pigeons on his head."

The concerto began, the young violinist Itzhak Perlman playing the solo with such skill and sweetness that it seemed a step beyond human limitations.

I noticed a boy of ten or twelve in a box below us. The moonlight was on his hair and shoulders. His eyes were fixed on Perlman, his hands clenched on his knees as he listened. I wondered if he dreamed of playing a violin like that some day. I wondered if my grandson would.

I wondered if he would know it was ten thousand times harder than walking on the moon.

Cristophe's first birthday party was held on a Saturday afternoon, and while it was to be mostly for his peers in the neighborhood, Denny and I were invited. I had never liked birthday parties when I was a boy, not even my own. They always produced too many tears and too much violence. But of course we had to go to this one.

Of all birthdays, the first is the most awkward. The honoree doesn't even know it's his birthday. It's impossible to buy a present for him. He isn't interested in anything he can't eat or break. In that respect a one-year-old boy is very much like a chimpanzee.

We decided to get him a swing. My wife went to Pasadena that morning to shop for one. I had to go out in the west San Fernando Valley on business. We agreed to meet at our daughter-in-law's house for the party.

"Maybe I'll stop at a store out there somewhere," I said, "and pick up something else, besides the swing, if I can find anything."

As it turned out I found myself in the neighborhood of Topanga Plaza and stopped to look in the toy shop. It was a busy day. No clerks were free to help me. I walked slowly up and down the aisles, looking for something that might engage the attention of a one-year-old and yet be sturdy enough to resist annihilation for a few days.

I picked up a football and gave it a spin in my hands. It felt good. A football is a beautiful object, and wonderful to touch, with its pneumatic tension and its pebbled surface. They don't smell as good as they used to, though, when they were made of leather instead of synthetics. I put it back on the shelf. Maybe in ten years.

Everything else suitable for infants seemed to be for girls. Women's liberation hadn't quite yet revolutionized the toy industry. They still made dolls and cuddly animals, objects designed to condition little girls for a woman's role in society as the stewardesses of love, warmth, and tenderness.

I saw a young woman looking at the hobby horses. She was pregnant and was pushing a stroller with a boy in it and had a small girl at her knee. It occurred to me that she might be a lot more help to me than a clerk. I could lean on her experience.

The hobby horses were made of hollow plastic. They were suspended on steel springs supported by a framework of metal tubing. They weren't as charming and sturdy-looking as the old wooden hobby horses used to be on their wooden rockers.

The woman put a hand on one of the horses and pushed it tentatively up and down, testing the bounce. She looked speculatively down at the infant in the stroller.

"I'm afraid he might fall out of that one," she said to the little girl.

"How old is the boy?" I asked.

"He's just a year," the woman said.

"What a coincidence," I said. "So's mine."

The little group pushed on. I thought of following to see what the woman bought, but I was afraid I might be mistaken for a nuisance.

I gave up and headed for one of the department stores to look in the boys' department. I could buy the lad some clothes. I happened to see a pair of white shoes in the window of a shoe store. They had an air of sporty elegance. I went in. As luck would have it, they had my size. I'm rather hard to fit.

"I'll wear them," I told the clerk. "I'm going to a birthday party."

I'd spent so much time looking for a present that I was late for the party. It didn't matter. I hadn't been missed. All was disorder. The moment I walked through the door I was attacked by Stepan Bandera, their phony Labrador retriever. He went for my shoes. I gave him a karate chop and saved the shoes, but he got an ankle.

It was a good party after all. There was a great deal of merriment. The kid was fine—never shed a tear; busted his beach ball and fell into the cake.

Nobody noticed my new white shoes, though, except the dog.

As intimidating as he was, Stepan Bandera was the kind of dog a man could admire, and he reminded me that I had always longed for a dog of my own. My wife's poodles hardly counted. What I had in mind was a large dog that would sit at my chair, walk with me, ride beside me in my car, be a companion in my mellow years. I wanted a dog that was stout of heart—one we could take to our house in Mexico as a guardian, one that could deal with rattlesnakes and shadows in the night.

Then one Sunday morning I found a promising notice in the classified:

AIREDALE PUPS. AKC.

I had always liked Airedales, but never owned one. Their virtues were well known. An Airedale was loyal, courageous, and tough. An Airedale had pride. He was no lickspittle lap dog. An Airedale was a terrier, with a taste for the hunt.

The ad led me to a shady street of ranch-style houses in the San Gabriel Valley. I knocked on a gate. Looking over the fence, I saw a grown Airedale in the yard. He gave me a sample bark. There was neither fear nor anger in it: simple authority. Other Airedales trotted out. It was a chorus.

A door slammed and a woman came into the yard from behind the house, quieting the dogs. "What is it?" she called out.

"Are you the lady with the Airedales?" I shouted, realizing at once how stupid the question must sound, with Airedales all about her.

She opened a gate and took me back to the kennels to see the pups. There were only two left, not quite four months old, a male and a female. The female seemed to like me better. She trotted over and nuzzled my hand and stood at my knee. The male paid me no attention until I called him, and then he checked me out briefly and trotted off.

"I'll take the male," I said a minute later, wondering why. Perhaps I felt I was already outnumbered by females in the family. It was a choice, though, that I sometimes had reason to regret, in the weeks to come.

"Does he have a name?" I asked.

"We call him Pugsley," the woman said. "You can give him a new name though. It's just a nickname. The children gave it to him."

"No," I said, "Pugsley it is." I thought it might be bad luck to change a dog's name, just as it was bad luck to change a boat's. Besides, I liked it: Pugsley. It sounded like a dog. They hadn't let me name my first son or my grandson; at least I could name my dog.

She took me into the house to fill out the papers and showed me Pugsley's family tree. His sire's name was Fleetwood Superson, and his dam's was Fleetwood Sun Maid.

"Fleetwood," she explained, "is the kennel name."

"You mean I have to call him Fleetwood?"

"Oh, no. But you can, if you like."

I put Fleetwood Pugsley in the passenger seat and drove him home. It wasn't an auspicious beginning. He seemed to prefer the driver's seat, and I had to keep fighting him off. As we neared home, the misgivings began to set in. No matter how mature and experienced a man becomes, he never foresees the pitfalls of an adventure he is drawn toward until it is too late to turn back.

At the moment I drove up in front of our house the first of many unforeseen but foreseeable complications became apparent. The sound of my car had brought our two cats running from their idle occupations, and as I walked around the car to open the other door the little beggars were whining at my ankles.

I opened the door. The Airedale fell out. One cat hissed and ran. The other bowed up like a horseshoe and lashed out with a paw, claws unsheathed. I rapped her on the head with a foot and she scatted, hissing.

Pugsley was unperturbed. I took it as a good sign, though there was a chance it only meant he was stupid. I took him through the house and into the back yard. The poodles were waiting at the door, leaping about and yipping idiotically. The male poodle ran into his house. The female bared her teeth, frightened herself with a bark, and followed her craven mate into their disenchanted cottage.

That evening I made drinks for Denny and me, to ease

our tensions. Everyone's nerves were taut. The cats remained
hostile and furtive. The poodles cowered in their house, pros-
trated by fear and jealousy. Only the Airedale remained unperturbed.

"Don't forget," Denny said, "he's yours."

In the next few weeks the amount of mischief he thought
up was beyond belief. He visited one calamity after another on
us, dismantling furniture, shredding garments, peeling the
covers off magazines, polkadotting carpets, excavating some
articles and burying others, and keeping the cats and poodles
in a state of unrelieved anxiety, not to mention me.

His excesses seemed to me to go so far beyond the normal patterns of canine adolescence that finally I took him
down the hill to Dr. Morehouse, who had doctored all our
other dogs and was no stranger to psychotic behavior.

"I expected him to be frisky," I told him, "being a
terrier, but I'm beginning to think it's a disorder—maybe
something glandular."

Dr. Morehouse sat him on a steel table and thumped
him here and there and looked into his eyes and mouth.

"Good dog," he said. "Good temperament. Intelligent,
too, I'll bet."

"Intelligent?"

"That's one reason he's so aggressive. You should consider yourself lucky, Smith, to have finally got yourself an
intelligent dog—this late in life."

"I suppose he'll calm down then—when he's older?"

"Oh, yes. That is until the sex drive sets in. Then he
may get worse."

CHAPTER THIRTEEN

Driving down the hill one morning in December I caught a glimpse of Mount Baldy over the rooftops. It was white, and I realized that this annual vision of a snow-capped Mount Baldy was as close as I had ever come to a white Christmas. In fact I had rarely thought of that distant whiteness as being real snow on the ground, something that could be walked in and picked up and molded into snowballs and thrown. It was merely some clever illusion, another motion-picture backdrop, artificially created like the snow scenes out at Universal Studios.

Except for the seasonal mantle on Mount Baldy, I saw snow only a few times as a boy and so it has no power over me. I am not persuaded that Christmas is more fun when the water pipes are frozen and you have to put on boots and an overcoat and shovel your way out to get the morning paper.

But on this particular morning Mount Baldy looked inviting, and I picked up my daughter-in-law and grandson and we headed for the mountains. She was *enceinte* again, and I thought she might find a ride through the snow exhilarating.

The road to Angeles Crest Highway was dry. There was hard snow on the ground at Mount Wilson. I made a snow-

ball and tried to hand it to my grandson. He hid his hands.
I realized, almost with a feeling of guilt, that he had never
seen snow before.

"Snow," I said.

He shook his head.

"*Neige,*" said his mother, encouraging him.

"What's that?" I asked.

"*Neige,*" she said. "It is snow in French."

We walked carefully out to the point and looked out
over the coastal plain. I could think of no comparable view
in the world. Where else could one look out at such a vast
metropolis from such a height? The spires of the new downtown skyline stood like a hub at the center of a wheel whose
rim encircled ten million people and their follies and fabrica-
tions, and vanished in the deserts and the sea.

"You can see your house?" Jacqueline asked.

Actually, I had once found my house from that point,
looking through a ten-cent telescope. But the telescope was
no longer there, and I could only guess at the spot with the
naked eye. What a splendid vanity, though, to look out over
that incomprehensible metropolis and pick out the mote where
one kept his books and his dog and got his mail.

We drove back to the highway and headed east. The
mountains grew higher around us and turned white. Now
and then a gap would open in the mountains and the plain
would come back into view, the way it will on a banking
airplane, incredibly close and detailed.

Then a gap opened to the north and there was the
desert; a pastel wash of pink and beige and blue, as endless
as the sea.

The skiers in their bright wraps were out on the slopes
of Holiday Hill, vivid against the snow. It might have been
some gigantic set on which a Grandma Moses Christmas card
was being brought to life.

We turned into Wrightwood and stopped at an inn for hamburgers and coffee.

"Donno," my grandson said when the hamburgers came.

"What's that mean?" I asked.

"He is saying hamburger."

"You mean hamburger is *donno* in French?"

"No. It is English. He is saying McDonald's. He sees the McDonald's commercials, on television. He thinks it means hamburger."

"My God," I said.

From Wrightwood we dropped swiftly to the desert and drove back through Joshua trees to the Antelope Valley Freeway and back to civilization, where children didn't know the word snow and thought donno was the word for hamburger.

After the Airedale chewed up the poodles' doghouse I knew I would have to do something about what had become an acute housing problem.

There was no putting the doghouse back together again. He had simply dismantled it, board by board, and chewed each element beyond repair. We were lucky to salvage some of it for kindling.

It was obvious there would be no point in buying another wooden doghouse, since it was likely to meet the same fate. I looked at various types of houses in a catalog at the pet shop, but they were all too expensive or too vulnerable. One had a tin roof, but the Airedale would have chewed out the sides and let the roof fall in.

I was putting it off, hoping to get a house built before the next storm came. What I had in mind was a duplex made of cement blocks with a galvanized iron roof. The Airedale could live in one side and the poodles in the other.

Two events occurred, however, to intervene in the

execution of that program. First, the construction men digging up under the foundation to repair some old earthquake damage stopped work for the holidays, leaving a mountain of dirt in the middle of the dog yard. Construction on the doghouse had to be postponed.

Then the rains came. We got home in the middle of the storm and opened the door to let the dogs in as usual. The result was disaster. The rain had turned the mountain of dirt into mud. The three of them raced past us like horses pounding home in the mud at Santa Anita. We shouted and screamed but the damage was done.

I threw the door open and ordered them out. They mutinied. A little rain and the brutes had reverted. It was demoralizing. Our tenuous relationship had broken down. We got them out by force, but the evening was ruined, as well as the carpet.

Naturally, I wasn't able to let them in again over the Christmas weekend, though their whimpering touched my heart. I kept in mind that one tends to oversentimentalize at Christmas.

Then the rain grew worse. The dog yard turned into a quagmire. When I looked out the window I couldn't even see the dogs. I fed them by setting their bowls out on the step and getting back inside and slamming the door before they could reach me.

It wasn't till Christmas Day that we began to sense that something mysterious was afoot. Now and then we could hear the Airedale barking but it sounded strange, like a dog barking over the telephone.

"He's in the attic," Denny said.

"Don't be silly," I told her.

Then we began to hear thumps, like someone dropping heavy boots on a floor. Then we heard metallic clunks, like the sound of balky plumbing. I started to get the stepladder to look in the attic, but I realized the sound was coming from the bedroom wall.

"Where are they, anyway?" Denny asked later, looking out the kitchen window into the dog yard. The dogs were not in sight. Either they were so muddy as to be indistinguishable from the mud, or they had escaped. Suddenly all three of them appeared out of nowhere. They looked quite dry.

"I've got to get at the bottom of this," I said. I put on my boots and rain gear and went out. They were gone again. Then the three of them suddenly appeared, dry as turnips.

I slogged around in the mud till I found the answer. It was really quite simple. The workmen had neglected to replace the screen over the crawl hole and the dogs had found the opening. They were living under the house.

Meanwhile our color TV had freaked out during the rainstorm. The picture turned snowy, distorted and unstable. It was a cruel irony that this breakdown should occur just ahead of Super Sunday. It was also ironic that the picture had been better than ever since we had hooked up with Theta Cable, thus bypassing our flighty rooftop aerial. At any other time of year I might have been in no hurry to get it fixed, but I didn't want to spend Super Sunday watching the Super Bowl game in a bar.

I phoned Theta Cable. They said they'd have a man out Friday, which was none too soon. Just before he arrived, though, we stumbled onto the trouble.

Curt had come over to work on the doghouses. He was building one for the poodles and one for the Airedale, so we wouldn't have to let them stay underneath the house again the next time it rained. I was afraid the Airedale might chew some of our water pipes. They're nothing but iron and copper —no problem for an Airedale.

"Would you mind crawling under the house," I asked Curt, "to see if everything's all right?"

He crawled under the house while I waited nervously outside, holding back the Airedale. I heard a whistle. He crawled out, dragging a heavily insulated line. Its end was frayed and gnawed, its copper core exposed.

"Here's what's wrong with your TV," he said. "The cable's been chewed through."

"Good Lord," I said. "What about the pipes?"

"They seem to be all right. He was working on the telephone lines, though. It's a good thing it stopped raining."

"What will I tell the man from Theta?" I wondered.

The question no sooner occurred to me than a van pulled up in front of the house and the Theta man stepped out in his spotless blue coveralls. He was carrying what looked like some kind of electronic testing device.

"You won't need that," I told him. "We've found the trouble."

He stopped short, looking mildly irked. He'd probably had enough of people calling up with emergencies, only to find out they had forgotten to plug their set in.

"Your cable's been chewed in half," I said, realizing I had made it sound like his fault.

"That happens," he said amiably. "Little animals get under the house."

"Yes," I agreed. "There's a lot of wildlife on this hill. We have raccoons, you know."

He nodded.

"And possums. They're something like a rodent."

"No problem. We'll put you in a new cable."

I heard a commotion. Curt was shouting. "He's out!" The gate was open. The Airedale bounded up. He made for the cable man and embraced him, leaving two muddy prints on his laundered coveralls.

"Of course," I said, wrestling the dog down, "it could

have been my wife's poodles. We've been doing some work and the men left the crawl hole open."

"No problem," he said, wiping at his blouse with an open hand. He crawled under the house with a roll of cable and came out fifteen minutes later.

"Now try your picture," he said.

He went inside and I turned the tube on. In a minute the picture came in—wonderfully gaudy, good as ever. I wouldn't have to spend Super Sunday in a bar after all.

We were not that lucky the next day when we had to call the plumber. The weather was back to normal. It was one of those fine spring days that drive us out into the yard, or move us to get things done around the house. Easterners who say we have no spring in Southern California have never spent a January here.

Our old friend Brownell dropped by for the first time in years. He had been ill, and was simply trying to take it easy, being content to contemplate the human comedy. In the old days, when our boys were small, he had often come by on Saturdays to have a beer with us and see what domestic life was like. He had been married more than once, but these unions had left him no children and no residual relationships. He had always seemed to consider our family life remarkable. Brownell had been a Stanford man, when Stanford turned out gentlemen.

When he drove up Denny happened to be outside under the kitchen window running the hose up the drain. Our pipes were clogged again. I was standing back far enough to keep from being splashed.

"Really!" Brownell exclaimed as if in astonishment, after alighting from his car. "It looks like nothing has changed around here."

He and I went inside. I opened some beer and we sat in the sunroom to talk. After a while Denny came in looking muddy and undone.

"It's no use this time," she said. "You'll have to call the plumber if you want to use the bathroom."

At that moment Doug drove up in his second-hand sports car with Jacqueline and Cristophe. Brownell had never met the former Mademoiselle Joyeux and her infant.

I introduced everyone and then phoned the plumber. There was no way out of it, with the house full of guests.

"Mr. Smith," the plumber said, "this is Saturday. It's going to cost you double."

"I know," I said. "But my wife doesn't work on Saturdays any more. She's liberated."

"I wish I could say the same," he said.

We were waiting for the plumber when Curt drove up with Gail Paolucci. With his mustache he looked like a member of Her Majesty's Horse Guards.

"Really," Brownell said. "It's Curt, is it?"

He had come by to borrow some phonograph records. We were all having a beer when Jacqueline cried out in theatrical dismay.

"Ah, Mr. Smith, your little yellow fish is dead!"

I looked in the tank. It was true. He was a yellow koi, one of my rarest; strong and intelligent and aggressive.

"Ah, well," I said, "I guess we can't dispose of him until the plumbing's fixed. Have to put him down the disposer." I had never believed in elaborate funerals for pets.

At that moment the plumber drove up in a red van.

"You're just in time," I told him. "We've had a death."

When the plumber went to work on the sink, Doug told me what they had come by for. They wanted to borrow my car. They were going up into the mountains and their car wasn't in good enough shape, as usual.

"Sure," I said. "Besides, you'll have more room for the kid."

"Oh," he said. "We were hoping to leave the kid with you. I'm afraid it might be too cold up there for him. Is that all right?"

They left in my car and Curt and Gail left in his with an armful of phonograph records. The plumber was out in the front yard digging. Brownell and I were talking about the impending Super Bowl when my wife asked me what to do about the diapers.

"Diapers?" I said. "That's not my department."

It seemed there were diapers to rinse, at once. It was urgent. But the bathroom pipes were still backed up.

"If it's urgent," I said, "why don't you put them out on the sidewalk and hose them off?"

"Ye gods," said Brownell.

It was rather an ingenious idea. Fortunately the plumber hadn't shut the water off yet. I was out on the sidewalk hosing off the diapers when Gribble came out of his house across the street, evidently to watch the plumber. He saw me. He crossed the street and watched me hosing off the diapers.

Finally, he said, "What are you doing?"

"I'm hosing off these diapers," I said. "What does it look like I'm doing?"

"I think," said Brownell, "I'll just have another beer."

CHAPTER FOURTEEN

Some animals, I've read, can be fooled by experiments in which their environment is altered. Thus, if you put a bear in a cold dark room he thinks it's winter and begins to hibernate. Our springlike weather held; and on Super Sunday, as the temperature rose to the high eighties, my system evidently was fooled, like the bear's. I thought it was spring. For a while on Sunday morning I was actually irrational. I had an irresistible urge to go down to the garage and clean it out again.

"What about the Super Bowl?" my wife asked.

"I really don't care that much," I said. "What kind of man could sit in front of the tube on a day like this? It's a betrayal of the senses."

It was ten o'clock when I went down to the garage. It gave me a strange, heady feeling. I had triumphed over indolence and addiction. I wasn't going to spend a rare day like this in my chair, watching the little toy men play football in a darkened house.

I stood a minute on the front porch, absorbing the day. It was like a gift. The sky was the color of Montana's in June. The air was pure and balmy. The mountains were white over the rooftops.

I walked down to the garage and opened the door. I

stared in. The disorder was stunning, like a physical blow. It looked like a museum set up to illustrate the materialistic glut in which mid-century Americans had lived. It was a little Sargasso Sea in which we had collected the flotsam and jetsam from the mainstream of the Gross National Product.

How many times over the years had I faced this Herculean task? A dozen? Twenty? Each time thinking it would be the last, that the job was done; I could retire. But always afterwards there was some calamity that struck like the Johnstown flood, wiping me out.

Had we needed all this junk? There was my electric lawnmower, the orange paint still new-looking under the dust. How many times had I used it? Half a dozen? The power saw, still red and silver, like a Christmas toy cast aside. The files and boxes and trunks. The piles of dusty books.

The job had never seemed more awesome. It wasn't only that the physical effort would be prodigious. What really cowed me was all the decisions I'd have to make. What could be thrown away? What must be saved? Cleaning out a garage is finally an ordeal of agonizing judgments.

Unfortunately, I had let the Airedale in the back door of the garage during the rain and he had got into the box of clothes and remnants Denny had put aside for the Goodwill. Old dresses and swimsuits and bits of cloth were festooned about like pennants; some hanging from the old barbecue, some from the old sofa, some from the bookcase, and one strip of cloth, like a piece torn from a matador's cape, hung from the horn of Doug's old saddle. The dog had also scattered dozens of old shoes about, and old newspapers and magazines, especially the *Intellectual Digest*, for which he seemed to have a predilection.

There were so many seashells and bits of driftwood about that one might have thought we had stumbled upon some windward beach left high and dry by the ebb tide.

Denny had gone through a shell and driftwood period a while back and harvested her treasure from the little cove below our house in Baja, which seems always to be replenished by a tireless sea.

"It looks hopeless," she said. She had come down from the house, ostensibly to help, but actually, I knew, to guard her treasures.

She began picking up old clothes. She held a yellow skirt to her waist. "I think I might be able to do something with this," she said.

It was the same old story. Every time we had gone down to the garage to get rid of the impedimenta of the years, she had weakened, and behind my back the castoffs were retrieved.

We wrestled the barbecue and a garden table out of the way and I saw two cartons of big books, long forgotten. I slipped one out. It was Volume XVI of my complete set of the 1892 edition of *Enyclopaedia Britannica*.

"My God," I said, blowing the dust off the leaves and riffling through the closely printed pages with their wonderful engravings. "Do you realize that when these books were printed Victoria was still Queen?"

"Why keep them?" she asked. "Aren't they terribly out of date?"

"Are you serious?" I said. "They're not out of date for anything that happened before 1892."

In the old plywood wardrobe closet the boys had used in their bedrooms I found a row of Curt's uniforms from the recent war and my forest-green Marine Corps blouse from World War II.

"I didn't know I'd saved that," I said.

"Don't you remember? The last time you cleared out the garage you said everything had to go, but we compromised. You kept your blouse and I kept my wedding gown."

I saw a stack of old school papers in a ruptured card-board carton. I reached down and picked up a handful. They were book reviews, handwritten by one of the boys. *Cannery Row, Bridge of San Luis Rey, The Red Badge of Courage.* I felt a stab of envy for a lad reading those books for the first time.

Then I came to a theme, carefully typewritten, a dozen pages long. It was evidently a term report; a matter of the greatest weight. The title was typed across the first page in capital letters:

HENRY THOREAU'S CRITICISM OF A MATERIALISTIC SOCIETY

I sat down on a sack of cement and began to read. I read it through. He had stated his thesis in the final paragraph:

"Thoreau accuses us of trying to solve the problems of life by making them more complicated than they are. It is true. Our lives are cluttered with things that we accumulate trying to find happiness and comfort. I think, as Thoreau did, that we would be happier and our lives would be better if we pursued only the real necessities of life, which in his words are 'food, shelter, clothing and fuel.' "

"No use trying to do it all today," I said. "It isn't that important."

We went back to our shelter and I turned on the Super Bowl game.

"Would you mind getting me some cheese and crackers and a beer?" I said. "The game's already started."

"Is that all you want?"

"Yes. My needs are simple."

I was content. I had food, shelter, clothing, and the Super Bowl.

A few weeks later we went to Pan-Pacific Auditorium on a rainy Sunday morning for the winter boat show. The Super Bowl always leaves me surfeited with spectator sports, and I yearn briefly for some other diversion; something that will get me out of my chair and into the sunlight.

"It's a good time to go," I said as we drove out the Hollywood Freeway in a cloudburst. "There won't be any crowd."

The parking lot was nearly full; there was a big line at the ticket gate; and inside, the boats and yachts and aisles were a-crawl with landlubbers.

"People must be crazy," I told my wife, "to come out in the rain like this to look at boats."

"Yes."

We had been going to the boat show for fifteen years, at least. I had never bought so much as a dinghy. Somewhere along the line I had suddenly realized I was never going to buy a boat, but I kept going to the show, perhaps only to check the condition of my fantasies.

I even noticed a change in them. This Sunday, it occurred to me, though the larger boats were larger than ever, I was looking at the smaller ones.

"That's funny," I said. "Everybody else is stepping up in class, and I'm stepping down."

"You're maturing," she said.

I supposed that was it. I'd learned to cut my fantasies down to size.

I wondered about the others. What kind of people went to boat shows? There were the usual weekend salts; grizzled men with sunburned faces wearing double-breasted blazers with brass buttons and yachtsman's caps; trying to look a bit like Spencer Tracy or Humphrey Bogart. I was glad I had decided not to wear my captain's cap.

There were droves of young couples dragging toddlers. They hadn't learned yet. They trooped up wooden steps to peek down into the lounges of enormous cabin cruisers, far beyond their immediate horizons; or tried the deck chairs on houseboats that would have awed the King of Egypt.

Then there were the seasoned middle-aged: affluent and sensible, but still touched with old dreams. Outdoor people at heart; romantic people. Blue-water sailors who lived in concrete towers and worked in other concrete towers and never went to sea.

There were the usual speedboat nuts, and fishing nuts, and water skiing nuts, and sailboat nuts. We drifted along with them. I wondered what kind of nuts *we* were.

LEARN TO SAIL! a sign exhorted. WIN A FREE SAILING LESSON!

What could be more useless, I thought, than one sailing lesson; it might even be fatal. As a small boy I had had one violin lesson. My family suffered for months afterward, until I gave my violin to a cousin.

FANTASY BOATS, said another sign. I liked that. At least they were honest about it.

We moved into one of the big tents. The auditorium was no longer big enough to hold the show. It had expanded outdoors to contain our fantasies. Suddenly the air was full of bubbles. They were coming from a bubble-making machine on the bow of a great cruiser. They popped out of the machine and floated out over the crowd: iridescent, perfectly round, the most exquisite and fragile of nature's toys.

The cruiser's white hull shone in the house lights as if it were sailing through the sky. It dwarfed the men who stood below, looking up at the flying bridge with watery eyes.

I knew what those men were thinking. They were at the helm, on a run down to Mazatlán, in a double-breasted navy blue wool knit blazer with gray slacks and a navy blue and gold yachting cap and one arm was around Ingrid Bergman who was in a camel hair polo coat laughing and tossing her head because the wind was blowing her hair and she didn't give a damn. Of course it didn't have to be Ingrid Bergman. It could have been Goldie Hawn.

SUPERDOCIOUS! a sign cried. It turned out to be the British sailboat booth. The British boats were lovely, with dashing names. *Alacrity. Vivacity.* The British have a flair for naming boats. *Resolute. Indomitable. Victorious.*

"You know," I said, "with something fast, like this little beauty here, *Alacrity,* we could sail down to our house in Mexico, instead of driving."

A bubble floated down, bright shimmering gold and blue, and hit my nose and was gone.

We have always loved rain in Los Angeles. It gives us what winter we have. It puts drama in our bland heavens. It reassures us that God has not forsaken us; the desert will be held back.

And now it is more blessed than ever, because it cleans our skies. It isn't only that the city looks washed. It looks new, as if a freshly painted set had been moved onstage from the wings.

Mountains that were nothing but a shadow behind a gray backdrop are suddenly front and center, sharp and three-dimensional. The metropolis that looked from the hills like a brown swamp becomes a mosaic of shapes and colors, shining and pulsing in the limpid air.

Even those of us who have always lived here are astounded by this sudden feast of scenery, so long hidden in smog as to have been forgotten. It strikes us cruelly, how much we've lost and how little we've cared.

One Saturday after a storm let up I went outside to look around. We had received the usual providence. The fountain and the dogs' water pan were full. The trees were clean. But the wind had blown the roof off the doghouse. The dogs were inside, wet and wretched.

I wondered whether there was much snow on the San Gabriels. We can't see the mountains from our yard or house. We're not quite high enough. But from our rooftop, I remembered, the view was superb.

I went down to the garage and found the aluminum extension ladder and wrestled it back up to the house. I worked it out to full length and planted it in the ivy bed and climbed up to the roof.

Very cautiously I stepped off on the wet shingles and sidled up to the peak of the roof. From here, only a man's height above our ceiling, I could see not only the tops of the San Gabriels, sprinkled now with snow, but the whole central sweep of Los Angeles. Dark clouds were drawn back and the city lay in a corridor of light, from the white shaft of City Hall to the low shining arc of Vincent Thomas Bridge, leaping across the harbor channel twenty miles away. It was beautiful; a panorama that transmogrified its tawdry details.

I was exhilarated, and at the same time depressed. What a foolish thing, to build a one-story house on such a site. Suddenly, looking out at this spectacle that was not quite mine, I had a superlative idea. Why not build a second story on the house?—or part of one, at least; a studio–living room in the sky, to bring this glorious view into our daily lives.

The plan began to shape up in my mind. I saw the stairway, curving up from the old living room; the open landing, the beam ceiling, the big windows all around.

I was hardly aware of the wind rising and the darkening sky. It began to rain. I clambered down the roof toward the ladder. It was gone. It lay shining in the ivy, blown over by the wind. I walked around the edge of the roof, sizing up my situation. In the rain there was no safe way down.

It was raining hard. I knew I needed help. I shouted for my wife. Evidently she couldn't hear me. I stamped on the roof. I stamped harder, grasping a pipe to keep my balance. Lightning flashed. It occurred to me that I could be electrocuted. Thunder clapped.

Denny was in the yard looking up, her face astonished.

"What are you doing up there!"

"The ladder!" I shouted, pointing.

She ran around the house and got the ladder up. Sometimes I'm glad she's strong. I came down. We ran to the shelter of the porch.

"What's it all about?"

I told her about the inspiration that had come to me on the roof; the idea for the second story.

"You'll be all right," she said, "as soon as you're dry."

CHAPTER FIFTEEN

From the beginning Denny and I sensed that Curt and Gail had serious intentions, and they did not keep us waiting long.

Any doubt about the outcome of their acquaintance was put to rest when she invited us to the home of her parents, far out in the San Fernando Valley, for Thanksgiving dinner. In American culture, a young couple who failed to marry after bringing their parents together at the Thanksgiving table would be seriously compromised.

So it was with that feeling of meeting a new set of relatives-to-be that we drove out to the Paolucci house. Like the Joyeux, Bernie and Mary Ann Paolucci had two daughters, Gail's sister, Bernadette, being also the younger. Thus, when we entered the Paolucci household, the situation was reminiscent of that first evening in Tours.

But this time I was on my good behavior. There would be wine, of course, or Paolucci's name wasn't Paolucci. But there would be no language barrier, so it was not expected that he would ask me to sample every wine of the Italian campagna as a substitute for conversation.

It was evident that Gail was very close to her family, and would remain so, which meant that they would inevitably become a part of our family too. If it was not wine, I wondered what common ground I would have with Bernie

Paolucci, or would there, perhaps, be none at all? We were no sooner through their front door than my concern evaporated.

Paolucci and I shook hands, but he seemed to be straining to hear a sound emanating from the door of what appeared to be a man's den, just off the entry hall. I recognized the sound: a crowd roar and the frantic voiceover of the announcer. He had the Ram game on TV.

"What's the score?" I asked.

"Dallas was ahead one touchdown," he said. "But it sounds like something just happened."

We moved into the living room for the perfunctory introductions and exchanges.

"Well, Jack," Bernie said, when the conversation lulled, "we might as well watch the game. They won't need us in the kitchen."

As we headed for Bernie's den, I thought of that great last line in *Casablanca,* when Claude Rains and Humphrey Bogart are walking arm in arm into the night, and Bogart says: "Louis, I think this is the beginning of a beautiful friendship."

Curt and Gail were married on a Saturday afternoon in the Presbyterian Church of Pasadena. They were not members of the congregation, but the church is English Gothic, in gray stone, and they chose it for its beauty.

I was almost late, which would have been embarrassing, since being on time is the last of my virtues I can boast of as intact. Denny was waiting for me on the steps, looking like a woman who has just begun to worry. She had gone ahead of me, in her own car, to take Doug a white shirt. He was to be the best man, of course, and at the last minute discovered that a white shirt was not in his wardrobe.

"I was beginning to wonder," she said. "Everyone's already seated."

We entered the church and an usher, one of Curt's college friends, took her arm and led her into the wedding chapel and down to a pew at the front. I followed, feeling unnecessary. A man is always upstaged at a wedding—even the bridegroom.

It was a simple vaulted Gothic chapel with oaken beams and panels. Sunlight filled it softly through stained-glass windows. All was ready. Suddenly there was a burst of organ music, something antique and exuberant, pierced with joyous trumpeting. It was heraldic music, the music of beginnings.

The minister walked out to the altar, looking like a proper Edwardian baronet in his gray suit and his trim brown beard. Like the music and the church, he had been their choice, the Reverend John Wareham, a Unitarian of free spirit. He had been the minister at another wedding we had attended one windy day on Point Dume. The ceremony had been held in the open, in a garden by the sea, and he had worn an open shirt and read from e. e. cummings.

The bridegroom and the best man took their places, and I noticed that Douglas was wearing a blue shirt after all. Perhaps the white one hadn't fit. At least his shoes didn't squeak.

The bridegroom's shirt was red, one more touch of the unorthodox that seemed to characterize this ceremony, although the setting was richly traditional. How handsome he was, I realized, with steadfast eyes and a mustache of a baroque fullness and panache that my own lip, in my youth, had never been able to produce. He turned and looked up the aisle.

The bride was approaching on her father's arm, walking behind her sister. Gail's gown was white and traditional, but the veil was off her face. Her eyes were dark but full of light.

She smiled without self-consciousness, as if from sheer delight. It was a Neapolitan look, I thought. She was a true Paolucci, soon to be a Smith.

Music filled the chapel like a sunburst. It was Bach, I supposed, if Curt had chosen it. Or perhaps it was something older—something from the Renaissance. It was stately, yet light as a flight of bees.

Her father surrendered the bride to the waiting young man and Mr. Wareham read some lines from a love song by Elton John.

Then, as Gail had wanted, he read from *The Prophet*, his voice supple and resonant, riding easily over the seas of Kahlil Gibran's poetry. It was a passage urging that love should be followed, that they should love one another but not let love become bondage; that they should keep their separateness in their togetherness.

"In these days of zero population growth," said Mr. Wareham, "not everyone is speaking of children as the natural outcome of marriage. But Gail and Curtis want children and hope that in due time they will be so blessed."

A few more lines, then, from Gibran, admonishing that they were to love their children but not try to make their children in their image; that they were the bows from which their children would be sent forth as arrows.

Then all of us in the chapel were asked to come forward and stand close about the bride and bridegroom for the ceremony of the ring and the vows.

"The ring?"

Mr. Wareham was looking expectantly at the best man. A silence fell. A hand went deep into a coat pocket, groping. My breathing stopped. And then—an eon later—the ring came up in the best man's hand, a sapphire flashing.

It is always the critical moment in a wedding, when the ring appears, like that instant when a jet of water in a fountain attains its peak, shatters, and comes glittering down in the sunlight. It is too late for temporizing, and those who might have spoken out against this union have been admonished forever to be silent.

The vows were made and the minister pronounced them man and wife, invoking the laws of God and California. It is an ending that always takes me by surprise at weddings, in its suddenness, the fullness of its meaning, and its finality.

We all drove over the freeways to an Italian restaurant in the valley for a champagne reception and an Italian wedding dinner. The wine was chianti, which doesn't look at all like cognac, but I was very careful not to pour it on the tablecloth.

Bernie Paolucci and I were happy men. It was a matter of record, vouchsafed in the ceremony itself, that time would bring him a grandchild. And I had reason to be pleased with both my sons. Even as they left us, they had enriched our lives: one of them had brought French cooking into the family, and now the other had brought Italian.

CHAPTER SIXTEEN

When Cristophe started to talk his Grandmère Joyeux, who had never ventured farther from home than Paris, flew to Los Angeles to see her daughter and her grandson. Madame Joyeux had recently lost her husband. Jacques had suffered a heart attack on his postman's rounds one morning, and fallen from his bicycle, fatally stricken. His absence, following upon the departure of her daughters, one to America, the other to Paris, had kindled in Madame Joyeux an understandable desire to get acquainted with her only grandchild.

In thinking that I had been prepared for her visit by my exposure to Jacqueline and Nanette, however, I seriously overestimated the fruits of that experience. I was soon to realize that since our first meeting at the Joyeux home I had learned almost no French, and Madame Joyeux had learned no English whatever. Our language barrier was all but impenetrable.

This was demonstrated one morning when I drove to Jacqueline's house to deliver a French poster I had bought for her bedroom, or *chambre*, as she called it. The poster had been an advertisement for a show called "Tournée du Chat Noir," a coming attraction at some nightclub in Montmartre. It was red, white, and black, and featured a magnificent black cat.

In decorating her chambre, Jacqueline had chosen stark

128

black and white, with touches of vivid red. I felt sure Le
Chat Noir was just what it needed. I had bought the poster
and taken it by for inspection. She was delighted. I had
promised to have it framed. She had hoped it would be ready
before her mother arrived. Unfortunately, though, it wasn't
until several days after the arrival of Madame Joyeux that I
was able to pick it up.

With that fine feeling a man has when he bears gifts,
I drove over to my daughter-in-law's house with the poster.
It looked splendid under glass in its thin black metal frame.
I rang the doorbell. There was no response. I heard Stepan
Bandera bark. I was about to leave. Then I heard a child
shout. My grandson. In a moment a shape appeared through
the amber Flemish window in the door. But the handle did
not turn.

Suddenly I knew what was wrong. Jacqueline had gone
out, leaving the dog to watch over her child and her mother.
She had no doubt given Madame Joyeux strict instructions not to answer the door. One never knew who might
knock at one's door in that neighborhood, and, confronted
by a stranger, across that language barrier, Madame Joyeux
would be confused, at least, and perhaps frightened.

What to do? I would have to let her know it was me.

"*C'est moi!*" I shouted at last, expending possibly one-
third of my French vocabulary.

A minute went by.

"*C'est moi!*" I repeated, somewhat louder. "Mr. Smith!"

I heard a commotion inside the door. The handle turned.
The door opened three inches. It was Madame Joyeux,
peering through the crack. We both smiled like silent screen
comedians. The door swung wide.

"*Bon jour,*" I said, expending another third.

"*Bon jour! Bon jour!*" exclaimed Madame Joyeux.

I patted my grandson on the head. The dog bounded

toward us from somewhere back in the house and leaped up against my chest, driving me back to the door frame.

"He's got his growth," I said, wrestling him down to the floor.

"*Comment?*" said Madame Joyeux.

"The dog!" I said. "He is a monster!"

"*Oui,*" she said, beaming down at the dog as if I had paid him a compliment.

"Goggie!" shouted Cristophe. I had hoped he would be talking better than that at his age, but I was gratified to hear a word of English, at that moment, infantile as it might be.

I showed the poster to Madame Joyeux. She nodded enthusiastically and expatiated upon it in French.

"It's for your daughter's bedroom," I said. "*Pour* Jacqueline."

She regarded me intensely, trying to get my meaning.

"*Pour la chambre,*" I explained.

Her eyes failed to light up. It must be my accent, I thought. Perhaps it was too Parisian for her. After all, Madame Joyeux was a provincial.

It occurred to me that a glass of wine might put us both at ease and improve communication.

"Wine?" I said. "Is there any wine?"

Madame Joyeux looked blank.

"*Vin,*" I said, though I knew it was not as easy a word to pronounce as it looked. "*Avez-vous vin?*"

I saw no comprehension in her eyes. I certainly would have thought a woman from the Loire Valley would know the French word for *wine.* I made the motions of opening a bottle and pouring and drinking. She had seen me drinking enough of it in her house, after all.

"Ah, *vin!*" she exclaimed.

I was pouring a glass of California rosé when the phone rang. I picked it up and said, "*Bon jour.*"

There was a silence; then finally my daughter-in-law's voice, alarmed: "Who is it?"

"It's me. Your father-in-law."

A long silence. "Mr. Smith! I cannot believe it! My mother lets you in?"

"Yes. I spoke French to her."

"You speak French? What did you say?"

"I said, *'C'est moi.'* "

"Mr. Smith! I cannot *believe* it! That is *excellent!* Wonderful! How are you getting along now?"

At that moment the dog had another run at me, giving me what the quarterbacks call a blind-side sack.

"Goggie!" my grandson shouted.

"Oui—goggie!" shouted Madame Joyeux.

"Don't worry," I told my daughter-in-law. "Your mother and I are drinking, and your son is teaching your mother how to say dog in English."

Later, as I was leaving, I turned to Madame Joyeux at the door and said, *"Au revoir."* There was no point in leaving without having used all the French I knew.

Madame Joyeux frowned and wagged a finger in reproach. *"Ce n'est pas au revoir,"* she said. "Gootbye!"

"Ah, *oui*," I said. "Gootbye."

That interlude strengthened my idea that one reason most men are baffled by the housewife's yearning for freedom is that they're unable to think of the house as a trap. They see staying at home as an adventure, and can't understand why their wives want to escape into the monotony of factory or office.

Late one afternoon in October I was reminded of what improbable and charming things can come to a man's front door. I was in my den in the declining throes of a fever, sliding gradually back to normal, when the doorbell rang.

It wasn't the evangelists. They work in pairs. You can hear them climbing the steps, and they pause a moment before ringing, perhaps awaiting the divine nudge. It wasn't the Girl Scouts on a cookie drive. They work in pairs, too, but they giggle and scuff and ring the bell with such unrelenting authority that it always reminds me of a general-quarters alarm at sea.

The ring came again. I couldn't remember hearing any sounds of approach. I was hoping my wife would answer it. Then I realized the house was rumbling and gurgling and I remembered that she had gone outside to run the hose up the pipes again. It was up to me.

I got up and lurched to the door and yanked it open. It had been out of plumb since the last earthquake and responded only to violence. I always yank it open anyway, to gain a psychological advantage over whoever is at the door.

It appeared to be a small girl of eight or nine. She had large blue eyes and blond hair down to her shoulders. She was holding a live snake, one small fist clenched around its neck. Its head bulged out at the top of her fist and the rest of it hung out, wriggling like a loose spring. It took the starch out of me.

"Can I use your telephone?"

"What for?"

"I have this snake."

"So I see."

"I want to phone my mother to come after me. I'm afraid if I walk home he'll get away. He's really strong."

"What's your name?" They come and go, in twenty years.

"Ben."

It was amusing, a girl named Ben, but nothing wrong with it. Lots of girls have boys' names.

"Ben," I said. "That's a good name for a girl."

"I'm a boy."

"Oh, of course," I said. "I can see you're a boy. What's the matter with me? I guess your long hair fooled me." I realized that was a faux-pas, too. "Not that there's anything wrong with long hair on a boy," I added. "I guess I thought only the older boys wore it that way, in their teens. At that age you can tell the difference between girls and boys by the —you know—secondary sex characteristics."

He nodded. "I met you before. You gave me a bag. It was Halloween, and my bag was torn."

I remembered the incident well. His trick-or-treat bag had come apart on our porch and I had given him one of my wife's shopping bags.

"Come on in," I said. He followed me in to the phone. He looked at the phone and moved the snake with elaborate care from one hand to the other. They both looked up at me. It was obvious he could not dial his mother and hold the snake. One of us would have to hold the snake while the other dialed.

"What's the number?" I said. "I'll dial."

I dialed and put the phone in his free hand. Evidently his mother answered because he told her where he was and asked her to come and get him. "I have this snake," he said. "What? ... Yes ... A snake ... What? ... Yes. He's alive ... Okay." He put the phone down. "She's coming," he said.

We waited on the porch. In a few minutes his mother drove up the hill in a station wagon. Ben said thanks and got in beside his mother.

"We'll keep it forty-five minutes," she shouted at me, and drove back down the hill.

How could a housewife find drudgery in a day like that?

A day or two later, when I was home alone, the doorbell rang again. It was afternoon, and the school children were on

their way home from the school at the top of the hill. I heard
at least two sets of shoes on the steps and porch, and then
the ring. It was extra loud.

I guessed it was a couple of girls. Girls ring a doorbell
louder than boys. I don't know why that is. Electronically, it
doesn't make sense. A doorbell either rings or it doesn't. You
can't make it ring louder by pushing the button harder. They
do it, though.

It's much the same principle by which a woman who
thinks the house is too cold will turn the thermostat up to 90
degrees, thinking it will heat up to 70 degrees faster than if
she merely turned it up to 70. You cannot convince a woman
that this will not work.

I was thinking about this as I went to the door to see
what the girls wanted. I tried easing the door open but finally
had to yank it. The house shook.

It was two girls, just as I suspected. I recognized them
both. They were not intimidated. They had nicked me several
times for Girl Scout cookies, and I supposed that's what it
was this time.

"What's up?" I said.

It was the smaller one who spoke. The other girl happened to be about the best cookie salesman in the neighborhood—maybe the best; and it was evident she was being held
in reserve, in case I proved difficult. They had me set up for
the old one-two.

"Could we pick a pomegranate from your tree?"

All I could do was laugh. I was surprised by the question. For one thing, I was so sure it was cookies, and also I
was surprised that they would come to the door and ask
permission to pick a pomegranate.

"I was laughing," I explained, "because nobody ever
asked before, if they could have a pomegranate. They just take
them."

I sometimes forget we have a pomegranate tree, until it is heavy with fruit. It was a volunteer, like our palm trees and our Chinese elms. It had simply grown up through the ivy on the north bank and I hadn't the slightest idea what it was until it revealed itself by bearing its first fruit.

We have always been sought out by volunteers. I don't know why that is, except perhaps that we live on Mount Washington, which providentially has kept some of its rusticity, and I imagine birds and small wild animals are wont to bring us seeds from elsewhere and plant them in our yard.

I don't know if that theory is zoologically and biologically sound, but it's true that most of the trees and shrubs around the house spring up without invitation and prosper without care. Sometimes I think Random Chance has selected our yard for the new Eden, but my wife and her once-a-week gardener keep cutting back His work.

The pomegranate tree is up near the sidewalk the children use on their way to and from school. Even though the tree has grown taller and filled out, they still have to take a step or two into the yard before they can reach the fruit. They can't quite reach it from the sidewalk. So technically it's trespassing.

But I don't care. It is my belief that the pomegranate was created to be stolen. It is red and tempting. It is sealed, and must be broken open. Its contents are like jewels in a treasure box, to be spilled out or plucked out one by one. It is the antidote for Eve's sin. Its theft from a tree by a sidewalk on the way home from school is an act of innocence.

I thought of telling the little girls about my theory, but I realized, just in time, that it might sound odd if they went home and told their mothers that Mr. Smith, on the corner, was talking to them about sin and innocence and stolen fruit.

"Help yourselves," I told them. "It's God's will."

CHAPTER SEVENTEEN

I am not what might be called gadget-happy, but finally, for what seemed to me a number of good reasons, I bought one of those machines that answer the telephone for you.

Too many times I have come pounding up from the garage to answer a persistent ring, rasping out my hello with the last remnant of my breath, only to hear the click of a wrong number hanging up or a stranger's voice asking if I am the man of the house.

I hoped to escape the sales pitches; the people who wanted to sell me six more magazine subscriptions or a new roof, or wanted me to put aluminum siding on my house or have my termites inspected.

The main advantage, I thought, would be the harvesting, when I got home at the end of a day out, or an evening, of all the calls that had come in during my absence.

The machine I purchased is simply a recorder that plugs into the telephone. You first put your own message on it, and when someone calls, the machine takes over after a ring or two, answers the phone, and delivers your message.

But taping the message wasn't easy. I didn't want to sound too formal or too casual. I wanted to be cheerful, but businesslike. If it was a sales pitch, I didn't want to sound like an easy mark. If it was a friend, I didn't want to sound rude.

I plugged the microphone into the machine and spoke

my message: "Hello. This is a recording. This is Jack Smith. He is unable to answer the telephone at the moment. If you like, wait until you hear the tone, then leave your message." I played it back. It sounded fairly good. A little halt, perhaps, with a stutter here and there, but it got the message over.

I dialed our neighbor Dalton. Mrs. Dalton answered.

"Is Dalt there?" I asked her. "It's me, Jack."

"Just a minute," she said. "I'll get him."

"No," I said. "Never mind. Just ask him to give me a ring when he isn't busy."

"He isn't busy now."

"Never mind. Just tell him to call me."

I hung up. In a minute the ring came. I picked up the receiver to eavesdrop. There was a click and the machine started playing my message. Then silence; and then the go-ahead tone. I wondered what Dalton would say. Suddenly there was a familiar buzzing. It was the dial tone. Either the machine wasn't working properly or Dalton hadn't left a message.

I phoned the Daltons again. Mrs. Dalton answered.

"Did Dalton call me?" I asked.

"Yes."

"What happened?"

"He hung up. He said he got a machine and he doesn't want to talk to a machine. Are you all right?"

I was wondering who else I could try when the phone rang again. Once again I eavesdropped. The machine answered and played my message. After the tone I heard a familiar voice. It was Curt.

"Who's that?" he said.

I turned off the machine. "That was me," I said. "I've got one of those answering machines. How did it sound?"

"Terrible," he said. "You sounded like you were reading something off the back of a box of corn flakes."

Maybe, I thought, I should have Denny tape the message. She had a resonant voice and enunciated clearly. I wrote a new message: "Hello. Thank you for calling the Smiths. We are unable to answer the telephone at the moment. You may wait for the tone, and then leave your message."

I thought it had class. I especially liked the "Thank you for calling the Smiths." It was the way the airlines answered the phone when you called for a reservation.

Denny put the message on the tape, and I had to admit it was better than mine had been, although Dalton still refused to leave a message. I suspected it was merely envy on his part.

For a time I wondered if the thing was really going to be of any use. Then one afternoon I came home and turned it on and got the message I'd been expecting any day. It was Doug. He sounded tired and harassed but happy.

"It's a girl," he said. "Everything is fine."

A girl! It was about time. We hadn't had a female Smith born into the family since 1907. I had been delighted with my sons, but I had always rather regretted not having had a daughter, too. There was so much I knew about life to tell a girl. I would hardly be able to wait for her to get through her Terrible Twos. They never understood me until after they were three.

"That's wonderful!" I said. "What's her name?"

There was a click and a dial tone. I had forgotten I was talking to a machine.

Her name turned out to be Adriana Estelle. So they had rejected my suggestion of Gabriele or Michele, if it was a girl. I had thought it would be fun to call her Mike or Gabby.

But Adriana was fine. I could call her Andy.

One weekend, after the baby was old enough to be left with her grandparents, Jacqueline borrowed my wife's car and

drove down to our house in Baja with three women friends
whose names, if I have them right, were Loren, Joanne, and
Maude.

"Don't worry," I told Doug, "the worst that can happen
is a flat tire."

He was to leave town on business, and since my wife and
I were taking care of both children, we had little time to
think about our daughter-in-law or anything else, for that
matter, until the phone rang at eight-thirty Sunday night. She
was calling from the border.

"Which side?" I asked uneasily.

"It is San Ysidro. We are here."

At least they were in the United States. She was sorry
they would be so late. The car had heated up on the dirt road
and they had cooled the radiator with ice from the cool can
and taken the radiator cap off and of course all the water had
blown out. They had waited and waited for help and nobody
came.

"What did you do?"

"We have a quart of beer so we pour the beer into the
engine and we drive to Enseñada and fill up the water."

There had been other adventures, but she didn't want to
waste any more money on the telephone. It was midnight
when she got home and it wasn't until Monday that she
called to tell me the whole story.

"Start at the beginning," I suggested.

It had been a nice trip down. They had found the turnoff
and driven over the dirt road without trouble and were just in
sight of the house when the car got stuck in sand and cactus.

"We cannot go forward because of the cactus and we
cannot back up because the wheels are spinning."

"What did you do?"

"First two *very* charming men come along in their cars
and then a *very* charming man comes along in a truck and

they take a chain from the car of one of the men and attach it to your wife's car and the other end to the truck and they pull us out of the cactus."

They had found the house in order, but for one dead mouse. That night a cricket kept them awake, but they found it under a table. "Don't worry, Mr. Smith, we put him outside."

The next day they went down on the rocks and gathered some mussels and ate some of them and used the rest for bait to go fishing.

"Did you catch any fish?"

"We catch *two* fish. One was a perch and the other one was pregnant."

"What did you do with the pregnant fish?"

"We put him back in the ocean, of course."

They had cooked the perch and eaten it, sharing it four ways. "I love fish, Mr. Smith, but I felt very strange. It was only half an hour since that little fish was in the ocean."

"Did you have any trouble on the way home, after you put the beer in the radiator?"

"Only in Tijuana."

They had missed the road that bypasses Tijuana and found themselves in the center of town, utterly lost and dismayed in that vortex of gaudy lights, unnerving noises, and macho drivers. They were on a one-way street and realized they were going the wrong way only when the motorcycle policeman stopped them with his red light.

"What happened?"

"He came back to the car and he said, in English, 'You know you are going the wrong way?' and we said we really did not see any sign, we were looking for the border and we got lost and we are confused."

"What did he do?"

"He *escort* us to the border. He was *so* nice. And the

other cars, they know there is a policeman in front of us, and they drive *very* carefully. It was paradise!"

"Anything else?"

"Oh, yes. The tequila."

They hadn't known you couldn't take liquor into California and one of them had a bottle of tequila.

"What happened?"

"The man at the border, he said, 'Follow me.' "

He led them to a trough, or fountain, as she called it, and made them pour the tequila down the drain. "It was so sad. There was a barrel by the fountain full of empty cognac bottles and Kahlua and Drambuie. You know what I thought, Mr. Smith? There is a pipe going from the drain up to the office of the men."

"But you had a good time?"

"Oh, believe me, Mr. Smith, we had really a wonderful time!"

It just proved an old theory of mine that nobody has more luck than babes in the woods.

One thing I didn't understand, though. How did they know the fish was pregnant?

CHAPTER EIGHTEEN

Sometimes I wonder if I haven't gone too far in giving up my traditional male roles in the interest of equality. In some neighborhoods a liberated wife is easily mistaken for a persecuted wife.

One evening my wife was out in the street raking up the leaves from the alder trees. There must have been a ton of them. Actually, I couldn't see why she insisted on raking them up. We have few enough signs of the changing seasons in Los Angeles. Who would know it was autumn, except for the leaves in the street and Monday-night football on the tube?

"The neighbors don't like the leaves," she said.

"That may be," I said, "but I don't see their wives out raking *theirs* up."

It was dark when she came in. One of the neighbors had come by walking his dog, she said, and told her he thought raking leaves was a man's job.

"What did you tell him?" I asked, assuming she'd explained about my liberalizing her role.

"I told him I needed a new rake."

"What did he say to that?"

"He said I needed a new husband."

"Don't worry," I said. "I have more respect for a woman

who rakes leaves than for a man who walks his wife's dog."

She wanted to get the leaves raked, she said, so she could drive down to Baja and spend a few days in our house on the beach. She wanted to get away and unwind and think. That night she packed our pickup and the next morning she got up early to leave. "Are you sure you'll be all right?" she asked.

I compared our predicaments. She was going across the border alone, driving over a hundred miles into Baja, the last eighteen miles over a bad dirt road, to spend days alone in a house that was far beyond shouting distance of its nearest neighbor.

She would be exposed to the chance of flat tires, field-mice, rattlesnakes, and the uncertainties of the night, without electricity or telephone, and with the wind rushing in across the bay and blowing through the roof tiles. Maybe there would be no fuel for the lanterns, no wood for the fire.

"You'd better take Pugsley," I said, thinking the Airedale could at least bark at shadows in the night.

"No, I'll take Jolie," she said. "You'll probably feel better with Pugsley here at home."

I knew a fair-sized Baja rattlesnake would swallow that runt poodle dog alive. But she was right; being alone at home, I'd like to know the Airedale was at my side.

When she drove off I was surprised to feel a slight sense of adventure. It is always a challenge to be left suddenly on one's own. I was alone in a big city; a man who had voluntarily weakened his ability to cope by surrendering too many of his male prerogatives.

Actually, I had no problems. I've always been a tidy man in a kitchen. We had ants, though, and I'd forgotten what one does about ants. Also, I felt a bit uneasy after dark; I was glad she had left me the dog.

Meanwhile, I reflected on her conversation with the

neighbor. Maybe I had been a little thoughtless. Even a liberated woman needs support. I decided to make it up to her. When she came home, she would find a brand-new rake waiting for her in the garage.

I did buy the rake that weekend, but it was some time before she was able to use it. I was gone from the house most of that Saturday and when I returned home I phoned Curt to see if she had called. I always worried about an emergency.

"We've been trying to get you," he said.

"What is it?"

"Mother phoned."

So something had happened. He was giving it to me a step at a time.

"What is it?"

"She broke her leg."

Early the next day we drove down to bring her home. She had slipped on a rock in the tide pools below our house and broken her right leg above the ankle. Our neighbors the Millards had been with her. They had helped her up the cliff and driven her into Ensenada, more than an hour away, with part of it over a very bad road, and now her leg was in a cast.

On the way back I told her about the rake, to make her feel better.

"Not very good timing," she said.

"Don't worry," I said. "You'll be using it in no time."

Having a broken leg, I found out, isn't altogether a drag. There's a certain humor in it, as long as one knows it's only temporary, and that soon enough one will be on his feet again.

At the beginning I rather enjoyed the novel responsibility of doing the cooking for the two of us. I found it easy enough to keep house and hold a job, though I certainly wouldn't have wanted small children underfoot. Maybe someday, but not just yet.

Meanwhile, Denny took to her bed. She was obliged to keep the broken limb elevated for the time being. It was encased in an enormous cast put on by the doctors in Ensenada, and it took a great deal of energy, evidently, to swing it around.

She was learning to walk, though, on the pair of crutches I had picked up at the local Thrifty drugstore. It was the only place I could find open the night we brought her back from Mexico. They were perhaps not the best crutches made, but we agreed there was no use spending much on something one would be only too glad to cast aside before long.

She did have a hard time voting. She hadn't learned to go up and down stairs yet, without sitting down and taking the steps on her seat. That was how she had gotten off the rocks and up the steps from the beach after breaking her leg, backing all the way up the cliff, with the fractured limb held out like a tea drinker's finger.

It was also how she got up the steps to the polling place on election day. Watching her tortured ascent, undignified but doughty, with the American flag hanging in the background, I was moved by a feeling that here in the flesh was the unquenchable democratic spirit.

We were fortunate, at this period, for the presence of our new daughter-in-law Gail, the former Miss Paolucci. It wasn't only that she understood football and basketball, and that her lasagna had more than gratified my expectations, but also she was now a graduate physical therapist, and it was she who taught Denny how to walk on crutches and get her exercise.

Unfortunately for my hope of liberation, though, Gail had found a position in the physical therapy department of a hospital, and had little time to do more than work with my wife briefly on her occasional calls. Much as I would have enjoyed turning the kitchen over to her, I had to carry on by myself.

The most difficult part was planning the menus. It wasn't simply a matter of throwing something in the pan and opening the beer. I tried to provide a balanced diet, high in protein, without forgetting that the food must be tasty, as well as nourishing, and the plate attractive.

One day I bought some frozen fish. I have never found a decent frozen fish, but I wanted something high in protein and low in carbohydrates and took a chance. There were four squares of fish in the package. They looked like laminated cardboard. With faint hope I followed the directions, brushing butter on each square and sticking them in the oven at 425 degrees.

I prepared a package of frozen cauliflower in cheese sauce and dismembered a head of lettuce and served the fish with slices of lemon. The results were quite attractive, the color scheme green and yellow, with one tiny red tomato on each plate for a vivid contrast.

I turned the lights low and opened the window by the dining-room table to let the evening air in, after the heat of the day. In a moment the Airedale had his forepaws on the sill and his head in the window, looking in. I had long since taken down the screen to improve the view.

I took a bite of my fish. Then, one at a time, I tossed the pieces out the window. The Airedale vanished. A moment later I looked out the window and the fish was gone.

Fortunately we didn't have to rely on my cooking alone. People were so kind after Denny broke her leg that I think the restoration of our belief in human goodness was worth the price.

Our neighbor Mrs. Dalton phoned one day to say she was coming over that night with a jar of chicken soup and a pot of boeuf Bourguignon, along with Dalton. Mrs. Dalton is the only person I know who puts chicken soup up in jars and drives it around to ailing friends.

"Will it help a broken leg?" I asked.

"Don't worry. It's the greatest wonder drug of all time."

When the Daltons arrived that evening I opened some whisky and got out a bottle of soda water to make some highballs. But I couldn't twist the cap off. It was frozen fast.

"Use your nutcracker," said Dalton.

I pointed out that I hadn't been able to find the nutcracker since our French daughter-in-law washed the dishes on Thanksgiving Day.

"Let me try it," said Mrs. Dalton. I slid the bottle to her over the bar. I knew she wasn't going to do it, if I couldn't. She put the cap of the bottle between her molars, bit down, twisted, and made a face. The cap came off.

"My God," I said. It was a feat I had never seen a woman do.

Later I opened a bottle of blanc de blanc and we dined. The boeuf Bourguignon was excellent. But I kept thinking how good it would be the next day. Mrs. Dalton is one of those cooks whose leftovers are better than the original dinner.

After dinner she marched into the kitchen to do the dishes. By rhetoric and force, I got her out. "Other people doing the dishes," I pointed out, "is why I can't find the nutcracker."

On Saturday Jacqueline phoned to say she was coming over to cook dinner for us that night.

"What are we having?" I asked.

"*Blanquette de veau.*"

I had the feeling I had become busboy and dishwasher in a French restaurant.

She arrived at eight-thirty with a sack of groceries, our

grandson, and our infant granddaughter, Adriana, and set to work in the kitchen. I tried to keep an eye on the kid. He was pushing three and like the Airedale was somewhat less wantonly destructive than he had been a year before. But he maneuvered better, and was swifter and more selective.

First he faked me out with a bit of exemplary behavior, and when I looked next he was emptying a half-gallon carton of milk on the Rampur rug. As his mother and I were on our knees sopping it up with sponges, we heard a cry from my wife. The kid had come out of the bathroom with lipstick up to his elbows.

His mother leaped up. "My dinner!" she shrieked, dashing for the kitchen. Her *blanquette de veau* was boiling over.

"The baby's crying," Denny said, looking at me. "She wants her bottle."

"I have to feed the dogs," I said.

I was scrubbing the lipstick off the kid's arms when I heard another scream from my wife. The Airedale had got in.

"Goggie!" shouted the kid.

"My crutch!" Denny shouted. "He's got my crutch."

"Dinner is ready!" cried Jacqueline.

We were all too excited to eat, but I opened a new bottle of blanc de blanc and soon had myself tranquil.

I forebade Jacqueline to wash the dishes. It ordinarily takes a week to find everything after she washes our dishes, and some things, like the nutcracker, are never seen again. She insisted, no doubt needing to ease her feelings of guilt over the spilled milk.

The next day Denny and I spent alone. I had planned Sunday dinner around a can of kosher stuffed cabbage, but I couldn't find the can opener.

"I guess we'll have to have the chicken soup," I said.

"What about the dogs and cats?"

There turned out to be enough of Mrs. Dalton's wonder drug, thank God, for the seven of us.

CHAPTER NINETEEN

By the time Nanette was able to visit us a second time, she had a niece as well as a nephew, and she herself had acquired the polish of a year's residence in Paris, though it had not, I soon found out, done much for her English.

She was training to be a nurse; but her studies, while arduous, did not include the English language, and she had no one, among her friends, to practice it with.

Meanwhile, my own progress in French had been even less remarkable. My daughter-in-law's English was improving every day, though her accent remained as baroque as the Paris Opera, and we simply did not make the effort to speak French. I felt stupid, having no facility in a language that was now a part of my family's heritage; but it was much easier and safer, for me, to stay with English.

Anticipating Nanette's next visit, however, I had obtained a booklet on Los Angeles, published by the American government in French, for French tourists contemplating an exploration of our city. Though I couldn't read French, I could of course make out a good many of the words, and it occurred to me that Los Angeles somehow sounded more romantic and sophisticated when described in that romantic language.

In the same way, I have noticed, we are likely to imagine

that a person with a French accent, especially a woman, is more sophisticated than one with a Brooklyn accent. I don't know why this should be so. Brooklyn, if you throw in its sister boroughs, has just as good schools and libraries as Paris.

But French has always been advertised as the main instrument of civilization, especially by the French; and so to the American ear, used to the twang of Babbitt, even the most banal of thoughts, if expressed in French, somehow have the ring of silver bells.

For example, the booklet on Los Angeles mentioned the outdoor concerts and sings at MacArthur Park as the *"chant choral, au MacArthur Park, tous les weekends."*

Right there you may see what I mean about the French language lending enchantment to the commonplace, though I have some doubt about the Gallic origin of that word *week-end.* I have attended a few of those concerts in the park and found them pleasant, but like almost anything, they sound more palatable in French, just as *museau de boeuf en salade* sounds more palatable than salad of ox muzzle.

All the usual tourist sights were listed in the brochure under *Que Voir, Que Faire* (What to See, What to Do). I ran my eye down the list of attractions until it fell on Lion Country.

"Lion Country: Laguna Hills, 13 kilomètres de pistes à travers jungle où les animaux évoluent en liberté."

I recalled that Mademoiselle Joyeux had expressed a wish to see Lion Country. I decided to telephone and arrange to take her. Jacqueline answered the phone.

"Is Nanette there?" I asked.

"She is watching television, Mr. Smith."

"What is she watching?"

"It is a movie. It is all about love and money and hate and jealousy, Mr. Smith. All the things we adore."

"You are watching it too?"

"Of course. I must translate for my sister."

"This will only take a minute," I said. "I want you to ask your sister something."

"Of course."

"Ask her how this sounds. '*À travers jungle où les animaux évoluent en liberté.*' Got it?"

Silence.

"You don't understand?"

"Oh, yes, of course, Mr. Smith. I understand. You said *animaux* and *liberté*. The animals are on liberty. Yes?"

"It's about Lion Country," I said.

"Oh, *oui!*" she exclaimed. "Lion Country! The animals are on liberty. Of course. Your wife did that to you?"

"No," I said. "I did it to myself."

I let her go back to love and money and hate and jealousy and all the things they adore.

There were other listings that seemed to sound more exciting in French—*Jardins Descansos, Le Queen Mary, Croisières dans le port* and *symphonies sous les étoiles, Hollywood Bowl* . . .

Symphonies sous les étoiles. Yes, very pretty. But no lovelier a phrase, I thought, than symphonies under the stars. There was something to be said for English after all.

My inquiry about Lion Country was of course interpreted by my daughter-in-law as an invitation to take the whole lot of them, and a stranger as well.

She phoned me at the last minute on the morning set for the outing. "It is all right," she said, "if we bring Kyle?"

"Kyle?"

"Oui. He is the little boy who lives across the street."

"Oh, yes," I said. "Of course. The more the merrier."

Actually, I wasn't too sure about it. In a sense we were going on safari, and I was the responsible man; the white hunter, so to speak. When you're responsible for everyone's life you like to know who your people are; their strengths and weaknesses; their breaking points.

Jacqueline and Adriana rode up front with me. The baby was not much over a year old and didn't speak English yet; but she was given to shrill outbursts which evidently were expressions of either rage or glee, depending on her mood. In either case, I had reason to know, her scream could freeze a man's marrow.

Cristophe, Kyle, and Nanette rode in back. My grandson sat behind me, or stood, most of the time. Anyway, he seemed to be just behind my ear. Once I had been afraid he would never learn to speak English; by the time we got to Lion Country I wished he had waited another year.

We arrived, though, with our nerves intact; but when they gave us that warning to keep our doors locked and our windows up, I doubt if there was a man among us who didn't feel a thrill.

It wasn't that I hadn't known danger. I'd seen and done everything twice. The killer whales at Marineland; the dancing bears at Japanese Village. I had shot the rapids at Magic Mountain and come down the Matterhorn at Disneyland and flown to Catalina in a seaplane. But no lion is ever tame and no man—Frank Buck, Clyde Beatty, not even the best of us— ever gets over his fear of the big cats.

We were no sooner through the gate than an ostrich came alongside to gawk at us. Except for the vulture, the ostrich is the ugliest of birds; and except for the cassowary, the meanest.

"*Autruche,*" said Jacqueline.

"*Oui, autruche,*" echoed Nanette from the back seat.

"*O*strich," I said. "It's *O*strich. Not *Oh*troosh."

"Hosstrich," said Jacqueline.

"Hosstrich," said Cristophe.

We drove through clumps of animals which I suspected might be gnu, oryx, eland, and wildebeest, but I identified them all as antelopes, which sounds very much like cantaloupes, and everyone was able to pronounce it.

The lions of course were separated from the antelopes by a fence, and we all grew apprehensive as we passed through the gate into the real lion country.

Suddenly we saw lions; a big male and half a dozen females; his harem. It was midmorning and hot as Africa, and the lions were lying about in the shade of some palm trees, as indolent as house cats.

Suddenly the male got up on his feet and slunk over to one of the dozing females and made a rather basic approach. The lioness raised her head and snarled at him and let him have a paw across the muzzle. He backed off and dropped in the dirt with a sigh.

"She is not interested?" said Jacqueline.

"No," I said. "She has not read *The Sensuous Woman*."

I wanted to move on, but the people in front of us were taking pictures through their closed windows, blocking our way. I started to back up, so I could go around them. Suddenly Jacqueline gasped.

"Mr. Smith!" she cried.

I hit the brake. "What! What is it!"

"A lion!"

"A lion! Where!"

"In back of us! You are running over him!"

I looked in my rear-view mirror and saw the lion. A full-grown male. I had almost hit him. In a moment he padded on around the side of the car and stood within a yard of my window. I froze.

We never knew whether it was rage or glee, but suddenly

the baby let us have one of her high ones, right in my ear.

Cristophe turned out okay. So did Kyle and the others. Made of good metal, every man jack of them.

But we found out where *my* breaking point was, right then.

By leaning on some old loyalties, I managed to get my daughter-in-law and her sister onto the Twentieth Century–Fox lot one day, and as things turned out, nothing I had ever done, I suppose, made me look so important in their eyes.

We not only saw them shoot an action scene for *The Towering Inferno,* but also were received in his dressing room by a star of the first magnitude in deshabille.

At the gate I had given my name and the guard had waved us through. This alone, I imagine, was enough to establish me in the minds of two young Frenchwomen as a man of formidable connections. I didn't tell them I'd been in the Marine Corps with the studio publicity chief and gone to Belmont High School with the unit man.

I was heartened when the guard at the stage door knew my name. He had been briefed. "Follow me," he said with practiced goodwill. He led us to Don Morgan, the Belmont man.

We were on a cavernous set. It appeared to be a sky-scraper restaurant like the Top of the Mark. A circular bar at the center with a statue of three nude nymphs. An encir-cling terrace, and through the glass wall a panoramic view of San Francisco Bay.

But it was chaos. We had intruded at some desperate hour. Chairs and tables were tumbled; walls were charred; the carpet was awash. Three men in soaked tuxedos were lashed to a post. In the murk around the set stood men with haggard faces and disheveled dinner clothes. Survivors. Dead bodies were piled in an alcove.

We followed Morgan, picking our way through cables and debris. "Better not stand here," a man cautioned. "This is a lightning machine. It shoots out terrible sparks."

We took shelter. Someone called "Quiet!" The director outlined the take. "First the guns . . . then the lightning . . . then the water . . . then the debris . . . Everything goes on '*Action.*' Is the debris ready?"

Morgan explained: This is the one hundred and thirty-fifth story of the Glass Tower, in San Francisco, the world's highest building. Opening night. Fire has broken out below and is racing up the tower. Paul Newman and Steve McQueen have gone up to the roof to blow the water tanks and flood the upper stories.

A man walked around the set squirting smoke from a portable machine. "Quiet! . . . Action!" Two gun blasts. A flash of lightning. Terrible sparks. Water crashing down on the men. Debris.

It was over in a few seconds. It wasn't make-believe at all, I thought. It was some kind of heightened reality. Life is an accident, out of control. Movies are designs. The director is God.

Morgan said we were going across the street to the commissary for lunch, but first he wanted us to meet someone. We followed him up a stairway and into a sitting room. In a moment a man walked out of a bedroom. He was wearing only a white robe and socks.

He smiled, teeth very white, skin very tan. Twin bolts of lightning crackled toward us from electric-blue eyes. The very air seemed to vibrate.

"This is Paul Newman," said Morgan.

Later, in the commissary, my daughter-in-law could hardly breathe, much less eat with her customary gusto. But her sister seemed pensive.

"You aren't excited?" I asked her.

"Oh, yes," she said. "But I am afraid that in France when I tell my friends I have meet Paul Newman, they will not believe me."

A few days later, thinking Nanette might be homesick, and would enjoy a setting that made her feel at home, I took her and Jacqueline to a restaurant that was alleged to represent a French farmhouse in the time of World War I. It was the sort of thing we are said to do so well in Los Angeles.

The farmhouse stood beside the runway of Van Nuys Airport and was supposed to be the Headquarters of the 94th Aero Squadron, 1st Pursuit Group, U.S. Army, near Toul, France, in 1918. The house was bogus French Norman in style, with the plaster shucked off here and there, as if by German shells, exposing the brick. There were sandbags all about and a gun emplacement in front of the door. Bales of hay seemed about to tumble from an open loft.

Inside the door a hostess in a long gray Red Cross dress said there would be a wait and directed us downstairs to the bar in the basement. On the way down we passed through the squadron's operations office. There were orders of the day on a bulletin board, photographs of fliers and planes, and somewhere the ghostly sound of doomed young men singing "Here's to the Next Man to Die."

It was very dark in the bar, which was supposed to be the squadron's ready room. As our eyes grew accustomed to the dark an American flag emerged, hanging on a sandbagged wall.

"Does it remind you of anything, this place?" I asked. Nanette had been told nothing about the restaurant. She looked around, baffled. "It's supposed to be a French farmhouse," I explained. "In World War I. It's been taken over by the American aviators."

"It is look like Disneyland," she said.

Our call came and we started up the spiral stairs to the dining room, which was called the Officers' Mess. As we climbed we could hear the ghostly voices singing "Over There." I sang a few bars with the boys . . .

"You know that song?" I asked her. She shook her head. Good Lord, I thought. What did we fight the war for, if the French didn't even remember "Over There."

There was a portrait of President Wilson on the wall of the squadron operations office. "You know who that is?" I asked. Mademoiselle Joyeux shook her head.

"It's President Wilson."

"Oh, yes? I did not know he was so young."

I couldn't remember that President Wilson had ever looked young. He was just a face in my schoolbooks, as he must have been in hers. He just looked like scholarly old President Wilson.

I was glad when we were seated and the menus came. Might as well forget the war. But there was an authentic picture of the 94th Squadron on the back of the menu; a tousled lot, rakish but baby-faced, like schoolboys dressed up for a class production of *Dawn Patrol.*

"*Dawn Patrol,*" I said. "Did you ever see *Dawn Patrol?* It was a movie about World War I."

"I have seen, how do you say *On the West, Nothing Is Happen?*"

I wrestled with it. "Ah, yes," I said when I had it down. "*All Quiet on the Western Front.* A great movie."

A waitress came for our orders. Like the others, she wore a long blue skirt and white blouse with a red sash. "The waitresses," I said. "Do they look like French farm girls?"

"No," said Nanette.

"Well," I said, "I think they're supposed to."

"In France," she said, "the farm girls, they are poor old women. All the young girls, they go away."

"To Paris?"

"To anywhere. To get out of the country."

The first item on the menu was Burger Américaine.

"Your hamburgers in America," said Mademoiselle Joyeux. "They are a she?"

"Pardon me?"

"It say Burger Américaine with an 'e' at the end. Are z'hamburgers feminine?"

When we left the farmhouse the boys in the basement were singing—

> *I wanna go home,*
> *I wanna go home;*
> *O my, I'm too young to die!"*

The next time, I thought, we'd just go to a McDonald's, where the burgers were a he.

CHAPTER TWENTY

It is said that most injuries occur in the home, so I suppose I shouldn't have been too surprised that I hurt my arm watching television one night at Jacqueline's. Being in the neighborhood, we had dropped in to say hello and were seduced into staying for dinner by the aromas from her kitchen.

Doug was away at night school and Denny joined Jacqueline in the kitchen, so to entertain myself I sank into the living room couch and started staring at the tube. It was on, but nobody was watching.

Suddenly my heart thumped. The scene was familiar. I had blundered onto one of my favorite movies. It was Clark Gable on the screen, in his white hunter outfit, and Ava Gardner. Ava was in pants and a safari jacket, but nothing could conceal the grace of that long body.

The sound was too low to hear, but it was easy to see that the conversation was nearing a climax; then suddenly Ava was in Clark's arms; an impulsive thing. He shoved her away. No time for women here in the veldt. Then Ava gave him that slow, sly, devastating smile, and you knew she had scented the prey. I lurched toward the set and turned up the sound.

"You're watching television?" my wife said, looking in from the kitchen.

"Yes. It's *Mogambo*."

"*Mogambo!* Haven't you seen that—two or three times?"

"More like four or five."

"How can you take it?"

She doesn't understand. It's the genre. I have always loved high-humidity movies. The steamy jungle. The wild cries in the night. The long iced drinks on the verandah. The troubled sleep behind the mosquito netting. Alan Ladd in a limp white suit. Sidney Greenstreet delicately mopping his face under a revolving fan at the back of a nightclub in Macao.

"The trick is," I explained, "to forget how it turns out."

Gable actually orders Miss Gardner to leave his house, and she packs up in a huff and boards the riverboat. "Maybe sometime," he says, "I'll get to Paris. Look you up."

Suddenly I was struck in the left ear by a soft round pink sponge-rubber ball. It was the kid. He wanted to play catch. "Not now," I said, "I'm watching *Mogambo*. Don't you want to see the animals?"

He got the ball and hit my ear again. He didn't want to see the animals. He wanted to play catch. I felt guilty, watching a movie I'd already seen four times when my only grandson wanted to play catch.

"Okay," I said, picking the ball up off the floor. "Catch."

He was standing off to my left, but I found that I could keep my eye on the TV screen and toss the ball to him with my left arm, though it was rather an awkward movement, something like trying to roll up the left rear window of a car from the driver's seat. I once crippled my arm for a week that way.

Still, it went quite well. I'm not left-handed, but every basketball player develops left-handed skills, and I was getting it to him, my peripheral vision being almost as good as ever. His returns were more erratic. Some were true, and I one-handed them, as the baseball announcers say. Some fell in my lap. But most either hit me in the ear or went wild.

I was soon engaged in a more or less rhythmic exercise of getting up, bending over to fetch the ball, sitting down, cocking my arm, and throwing sideways at a ninety-degree angle to my left, all the while trying to watch *Mogambo*.

Finally Grace Kelly shows up. (Grace Kelly was the queen of humidity movies. No matter how narrow her escapes, how strenuous her exertions, how cruel the equatorial sun, Miss Kelly never lost her lovely porcelain facade. No bead of perspiration trembled on her upper lip.) And yet, when she looks up at Gable after he's shot the lion to save her life, there is the promise of something animal and reckless in those pale cool eyes.

The picture wasn't over yet when dinner was served. When we sat down at the table it occurred to me that my left arm felt hot and tingly. By the time I finished the wine it was numb.

"I think you'd better drive home," I told my wife.

What I had, I learned the next day, was tennis elbow. It may sound trivial, but tennis elbow is what forced Sandy Koufax to quit baseball, at the top of his career. In the same arm, too.

What really annoyed me, though, was that I still didn't know how *Mogambo* turned out.

My elbow was on the mend when Jacqueline invited us over to dinner for Cristophe's fourth birthday (I no longer called him Pete). I suggested that Denny buy the presents for him and I would pick up something for Jacqueline. It has been my observation that at small boys' birthday parties their mothers are at least deserving of a consolation prize.

The only gift I could think of was flowers. They're always in good taste, and even though a person may like daffodils better than marigolds, for example, it is hard to imagine a person actually disliking any kind of flower.

I explained the situation to our florist down in Highland Park. "What about some of these?" he said, showing me a bunch of pink, red, and white carnations.

I felt a surge of melancholy. Carnations always affect me that way. I suspect it's because when I was a small boy my mother used to take me to church on Mother's Day and if your mother was still alive you wore a red carnation and if she was dead you wore a white one. So every time I see carnations I think of somebody's mother, dead or alive.

"What about those?" I asked, pointing to a clump of big yellow chrysanthemums in a pot.

I have always loved chrysanthemums, especially the big yellow ones, so exuberant and bouffant. They are, after all, the flower of our most exciting festival in America—football. I never see big yellow chrysanthemums without thinking of football seasons of long ago, with the pink-cheeked cheer girls in their woolly sweaters and pleated skirts, shaking pompons and turning cartwheels.

"Those will last in the house for weeks, you know," the florist said, "and then she can plant them outside."

When Denny came home the pot of chrysanthemums was on the bar. I wanted to see her reaction.

"Oh, dear," she said. "You got those for Jacqueline?"

"Yes. Aren't they great?"

"They're very nice."

"What d'you mean they're very nice? Is something wrong with them?"

"Well," she said, "in France, you know, you only see chrysanthemums at funerals."

"Well, this isn't France."

"I know. But she can't get over the way she feels. She's told me. Chrysanthemums make her sad."

"That's ridiculous. It's time she got over those French prejudices. This is America."

That evening I was holding the pot of chrysanthemums when Jacqueline opened her front door. Her face fell. She is a transparent woman.

"Oh, Mr. Smith," she said. There was no joy in it.

"You don't like chrysanthemums?"

"Someone has died?"

"No one has died, for God's sake. Where'd you get that idea?"

"I am sorry, Mr. Smith. In France chrysanthemums mean there is a funeral."

I carried the pot in and set it on a table. "You've got to get over that idea," I told her. "In America chrysanthemums are a symbol of life at its most exuberant. They're the flowers of our most joyous festival."

"Z'Fourth of July?"

"Football."

"I am very happy no one is dead," she said.

After dinner our son took movies of the kid opening his presents and of all of us sitting around the living room with the pot of chrysanthemums in the middle of the table.

As we were leaving I offered to take the flowers home. "We can plant them," I said, "and I'll bring you something else."

"No, Mr. Smith," she said. "You are right. I must get over my feelings. Don't worry. I will write my mother."

"What do you mean—write your mother?"

"We must send her the movies, of course," she said, "and when she see the chrysanthemums in the movies she will think there has been a funeral. I will write her a letter and tell her nobody is dead."

The next time, I thought, I'd take carnations. If anyone had to feel melancholy, it might as well be me.

CHAPTER TWENTY-ONE

As a man who tries to turn all adversity to profit, if only the improvement of his own character, I emerged from a prolonged attack of laryngitis with a deepened respect for the power of the human voice.

Being temporarily speechless, I must admit, did turn out to have its compensations. It is amazing how many trivial questions can be answered with a shrug, a rasp, or a gesture in which the index finger is pointed at the open throat.

Also, without fear of inspiring hard feelings, the victim may decline a summons to the telephone. He may lie safely in his bed, eavesdropping as his wife tells whoever it is on the line, "I'm sorry, he can't talk. Yes. It's laryngitis." He is gratified at these moments by righteous self-pity and a sense of freedom.

Those small compensations aside, however, I did begin to gain a new appreciation of the voice as an instrument of command. Household discipline virtually broke down while I was incapacitated. I hadn't realized how much the harmony of our simple life depended on my spoken orders, even when they were disguised, humanely, as amiable observations.

This came to me one evening when my wife served a ragout of leftover beef. Finding it rather in need of seasoning,

I whispered, "Are we out of salt?" Ordinarily that would have sent her off to the kitchen. Instead, she merely looked up and said, "What?"

"I asked if there was any salt."

She leaned toward me. "What?"

I made a gesture of shaking salt in my plate.

"You want the pepper?"

By then I was on to her game. I could have brought her off it with a few words, but I knew they would have to be delivered with a tone of restrained but intimidating reproach. My voice wasn't up to it. I went into the kitchen and got the salt myself.

Oddly, it was the dog, with whom I was accustomed to communicating only on the most elementary level, that made me see how much authority I had lost. I was teaching him not to bark at trifles, and we had made good progress. Whenever I heard him start what sounded like a bout of senseless barking I needed only to switch on the outside floodlight, yank the door open, and shout "Quiet!" at the top of my voice. At this command, with its ring of mastery, he would lower his head and go into his house.

Something set him off that night, and, without thinking of my handicap, I switched on the light, yanked the door open as usual, and shouted "Quiet!" What came out was not quite as loud as a stage whisper.

The dog stopped barking but he didn't go into his house. Instead he bounded toward the door and leaped past me into the kitchen.

"Out!" I whispered. "Out!"

My wife staggered into the kitchen, sinking half to her knees in a paroxysm of callous laughter. "His master's voice," she whimpered, evidently overcome by some sadistic joy at my helplessness.

It taught me something. There was a touch of Delilah in the best of them.

Finally one morning, when I had reached the point where I thought I could feel my vocal cords vibrating again and could hear a slight, hoarse sound, I decided to answer the phone and try my wings.

"Hello," I said, sounding like a breather in one of those suspense movies.

There was a pause. "Allo? . . . Mr. Smith?" It was Jacqueline.

"Yes. It's me."

"You are all right?"

"I have laryngitis."

"What do you say?"

"Laryngitis. I can't talk."

"Mr. Smith, you don't sound like yourself. Are you all right?"

"What do you want, Jacqueline?"

"Mr. Smith, do you have some snails?"

"What?"

"I would like to borrow some of your snails."

It turned out she had suddenly been overcome by a hunger for escargots, but they were of course too expensive. So she had gathered some wild snails from her back yard. But there weren't enough. She wanted to come over to our house and gather some of *our* snails.

"Mr. Smith," she said, "you have hundreds of snails. I have seen them many times."

"My God," I said.

"What?"

"I can't talk. I'll call you back."

A day or two later Jacqueline came by with her children and a small kitchen pail.

"We have come for the snails," she said. "You are all right, Mr. Smith?"

I had forgotten her telephone call about the snails, or I tried to. It had only been a joke, or perhaps a hallucination, from my laryngitis. It was no joke. She was there, with her pail and her helpers, ready to plunder my backyard.

I shouldn't have been surprised. She was French. She was a good cook, the daughter of a chef. She was frugal. And like everyone else, she was squeezed by inflation. She had seen the snails crawling about her backyard in North Hollywood, fattening on her flowers, and said, "Why not?"

Her husband wisely had questioned whether it was safe to eat backyard snails, even if one had the stomach for such a dubious adventure. He had insisted that she telephone the Public Health Department. She had done that, though it was something she dreaded, trying to cope with bureaucratic English over the telephone.

"Zey say it is all right to eat zem," she told me, "as long as zey have not been poison."

"How do you know they haven't been poisoned?" I asked.

"Mr. Smith!" she said. "You would not poison a poor little snail?"

I let them go out into the backyard and they gathered two or three dozen of them, much to my surprise; I'd had no idea we were so well stocked.

By an unnerving coincidence, the next day happened to be Adriana's birthday, and Jacqueline invited us to their house that evening for dinner.

"You must promise me," I told her, "that you will not serve snails."

"Mr. Smith," she said, "I cross my heart. I will fix something else, special for you."

"I'm not joking," I told her as severely as I could.

Despite her promise, I had serious misgivings as we

sat down. However, I studied everything carefully before eating it, and except for a moment of uncertainty about the
chopped mushrooms, I felt secure.

Over champagne and birthday cake I was relaxed
enough to pretend a sophisticated interest in her snails. After
all, I might not be French, but I was not a barbarian, either.

"Just as an academic culinary question," I said, "how do
you prepare them?"

Somehow she made it sound like a Grimm's fairy tale:
"First," she said, "you go in the garden and you look for
snails. And if you find some little snails you wait till they
grow up and you put them in a box and you feed them for
two or three days."

"You feed them? What?"

"Spinach. *Salade.* Apple peels. Then you starve them for
two days."

"You starve them?"

"*Oui.* So all the stuff gets out of their body. Yes, they
must not eat for two days. Then at the end of two days of
starvation you put them into a big container of water that
is soaked with salt. So all the saliva and stuff gets out of their
bodies. You have to rinse them at least ten times in clear, cold
water. Because if you don't, they are still slidy."

"Slidy?"

"*Oui.* Slidy. And then you cook them for about forty-
five minutes in hot water, and when they are cooked you put
them in cold water right away and put them in your refrigerator, so when the water is cold, you take them out of the
refrigerator and then take them out of the shells."

I had a feeling that she had neglected the more repulsive
instructions, and pushed her for utter honesty.

"Oh. You do not eat the heads. You have to cut the
head off, and the intestines. The only part you eat is the part
that crawls on the ground. In the restaurants they do it with

just garlic, parsley, and butter. But me, I do it with a little touch of my father, which I think is much better; I put some bread crumbs in it, and I do something that nobody else does —I put in some Pernod."

So that was her secret. A touch of her father, and a touch of Pernod. The thought of Jacques Joyeux and Pernod brought on a twinge of nostalgia in me for that glorious night in Tours, when the two of us sampled the wines of the Loire. But it was not an emotion quite urgent enough to make me try snails.

CHAPTER TWENTY-TWO

My wife comes from Bakersfield, a prosperous small city in the fertile San Joaquin Valley one hundred miles north of Los Angeles, and though the heat can melt the streets in the summertime, we drove up in July for the annual family picnic.

There were at least forty people present, including our new daughter-in-law Gail, and it occurred to me that except for me and one or two others who had married in, everybody was either French, Irish, or Italian.

How they had arranged who was to bring what was a mystery to me, but I suppose the logistics of a major family picnic is a folk art that earlier generations brought with them from the Old Country.

I know that Gail took six dozen French rolls, which seemed odd to me, since I would have expected her to take Italian rolls, or perhaps a pan or two of lasagna. Anyway, they bake a very good French roll in Bakersfield, second only to the famous French rolls of San Francisco, and it seemed like coals to Newcastle.

Denny was responsible for the fruit salad. She got up at seven-thirty that Sunday morning to begin chopping her fruits, and it was only after she had already filled two gallon crocks with salad that I began to realize what a really big picnic it was going to be.

"Is that all we're responsible for?" I asked. "Fruit salad?"

"You could take some beer, if you like."

"Is your brother going to be there?" I asked. "And Danny O'Neill?"

Her brother Ernie was employed by a Bakersfield bank, but his capacity for beer, on weekends, was second in family legend only to that of Danny O'Neill, who also had a position of responsibility, in the city school district, but could put away more beer, pound for pound, than any man I ever knew, except for myself in my youth. Denny's older sister had married an O'Neill, thus bringing in the Irish wing, including Danny, who was her husband's younger brother.

"Yes, of course," Denny said. "They'll both be there. In fact I think the two of them organized the whole thing."

If her brother and Danny O'Neill were running the picnic I knew there would be enough beer for several days. All the same, one couldn't take such things for granted, so I loaded a case in the car, just to be sure we wouldn't run out.

We picked up Doug and Jacqueline and their children and drove up together, while Curt and Gail drove up with the Paoluccis and the French rolls. Mrs. Paolucci took a basket of Italian cookies, and Paolucci took a case of beer.

The picnic was in one of those pretty little public parks that used to make the summers endurable in Bakersfield when I lived there as a boy, before air conditioning. We gathered in the shade of some fine old sycamore trees, and began the business of trying to sort everybody out. There was a large galvanized washtub full of iced beer.

I had the feeling I always have at my wife's family gatherings, wondering how a nice lad of Welsh heritage like me had got mixed up with all those O'Neills, Sullivans, Bressons, and now Paoluccis. Once again I found myself reflecting on the fact that my line, which might go straight back to Welsh kings, for all I know, was being dissipated by these adventurous marriages. Of course I had started it by marrying a French girl myself; but how could I have known that one of my sons would also marry a French girl, and the other an Italian? It meant, the way I figured it out, sipping my first can of beer, that my two grandchildren were three-quarters French, and that when Curt and Gail had children they would be one-quarter French and half Italian. The Hugheses and Smiths were fading into oblivion, even though my name would be continued through the males.

Every contingent had brought a carton or cool can of food, and when they were emptied the resulting cornucopia of salads, chicken, and desserts covered two tables and took an hour and a half to reduce to leftovers, which were abundant.

After lunch the young and athletic among us set out to exercise themselves, while the serious beer drinkers like Ernie and Danny and me clustered under a sycamore and started lowering the level of the cans in the washtub. To my surprise, if not dismay, my wife borrowed a racket and announced that she was going to play tennis with Curt, though she still complained of twinges in the leg she had broken. Neither she nor I had been on a tennis court since the early 1960s, when a blister had forced her to quit for a while; we simply never had the initiative to take it up again.

From the shade of the sycamore tree I watched them rally. She is strong, quick, and well-coordinated, but she had never taken any instruction, except from me, and evidently I had failed to instruct her properly in the serve and forehand. Her backhand seemed to be instinctive. Curt hadn't played much tennis, I could see, perhaps because there were few courts for enlisted men in the Air Force. His serve was strong enough, but erratic, and he had no forehand at all. Reluctantly, I finished my can of beer and walked over to the court.

"You'd better get some help with that forehand," I told him. "The forehand is your basic stroke."

He walked over and held out his racket and a yellow ball. "You want to play?" he said.

"Oh, I'll just hit a ball or two," I said. "To show you what I mean."

The racket felt good in my hand. Though I'd never taken a lesson, I had played some in high school with a girl named Mary Frances, and I had often regretted not taking it up seriously, instead of pool. I might have been good enough for tournament competition.

I bounced the ball a couple of times and swung. The ball hit the wood of the racket and dribbled up to the net. Curt tossed me another ball. "You get two," he said.

I bounced the ball twice, to get my eyes coordinated, and swung again, giving it a bit more backswing. The ball reached the net on one bounce, but didn't quite make it over.

"It must be these yellow balls," I said. "I always played with white."

I began to get the hang of it, but my wife kept hitting them back. Then I got off a really superb crosscourt shot that made her scramble; she just managed to get her racket on it, and came up with a lucky passing shot.

"That's enough," I said, handing the racket back to Curt. It was foolish, I realized, to be playing tennis in the Bakersfield sun.

"Looks like you've still got your old form," Curt said, smiling.

On the way home Cristophe sat in the front seat between his father and me. I had got a bit of sunstroke playing tennis, and it was thought prudent that I turn the driving over to Doug. Cristophe amused himself, as we climbed the mountains, by counting out loud. He counted up to a hundred three times. It was having a hypnotic effect on me. I was afraid I might fall into a trance. But I didn't want him to stop. He might think up something even worse.

"I'm going to count up to a million," he said.

He got up to 109 and I thought I was going to have to stop him. My eyelids were growing heavy. But from 110 he skipped all the way to a million.

I felt better. The kid had a bit of the Welshman in him after all.

CHAPTER TWENTY-THREE

Toward the end of the summer we drove out to the San Fernando Valley one morning to see Cristophe through a critical rite of passage. We were to meet at Jacqueline's house in North Hollywood and proceed to the Kristenson swimming school for the ceremony.

Everyone was ready. The kid himself was already in his swimming trunks, which was appropriate, this being a land where life is casual and all of us worship the sun. We decided to go in two cars.

"We will meet you at the school," said Jacqueline. "We must stop at the florist to buy a flower for the teacher."

Cristophe went with them. My wife and I took his sister, figuring the kid could concentrate better if she wasn't along. I knew I could. We drove to the school. The teacher was waiting. She was tall and deeply tanned, with black hair and dark blue eyes; a Southern California Venus in her black bathing suit. Her name was Debbie.

The others arrived. Cristophe was holding a red rose wrapped in green florist's paper with a sprig of baby's breath. He handed it to the teacher with admirable savoir-faire for a lad barely four years old. She accepted it with grace.

"Are you ready?" she asked. He gave her his Robert Redford smile. They walked side by side to the end of the swimming pool. She got into the water and motioned to him. "Come on," she said. "Dive."

It wasn't a great dive. It was something more than a foot-first jump, though. He went in at an angle of forty-five degrees, head up. There was a splash under which he momentarily vanished. He came up swimming.

He swam the full length, kicking and stroking quite well, and turning on his back every so often to float and breathe. When the exercise was over he got out and his mother flung a towel around him, like a trainer throwing a towel around a victorious athlete. His teacher congratulated him and picked up her rose and we all said goodbye. It would be a summer to remember.

There would be other commencements, but this one was especially vital to a native son of Southern California, where it is the birthright of every child to be sun-tanned and buoyant.

Several weeks later we had the grandchildren with us over Halloween, and I was bemused by the discovery that our grandson seemed to have inherited one of my less enviable traits: he won things.

It has been my experience that anything a person can win in life is either worthless, a liability, or a menace. I am not talking about winning a game or an academic degree, but winning a prize, either by chance or through the exercise of some minor skill, such as being able to knock over a pyramid of lead milk bottles with a baseball.

This, it turned out, was exactly the sort of skill Cristophe had. Saturday night when we took the two of them to the Mount Washington neighborhood Halloween party at the playground, he did exactly that, knocking over the milk bottles with three throws and winning a spider. That the spider was only plastic made it no more desirable, and when he slipped it into his pocket, I doubted that I had seen the last of it. He also won a black pirate's eyepatch for throwing a bean bag into a small box and a plastic vampire bat for hitting a target with three darts.

As I say, this aptitude for winning prizes of dubious value seems to be inherited. I don't believe I had any extraordinary physical coordination as a boy, but I was crafty and lucky. As a result, I was usually in possession of something I had won, either vegetable, mineral, or animal. The animal ones were the most precious, but they tended to produce in my mother the symptoms of anxiety, if not hysteria. A woman, I know now, can stand just so many rabbits, guinea pigs, and chameleons; and so, I know now, can a man.

Having had that experience, I should not have been caught off guard Sunday morning when I headed through the house toward the kitchen to put the coffee on. I came across the spider on the new carpet. "It is only a plastic spider," I reassured myself, stepping over it.

But I had forgotten the goldfish. Cristophe had acquired the goldfish at an earlier party on Saturday afternoon at his sister's nursery school. My wife had brought the fish home in a plastic sack and transferred them to a peanut-butter jar, a procedure I observed with a sense of having been through it before.

I had had it with goldfish. It had started just like that, as I remembered, with a pair of the pretty little nippers the boys brought home in a sack, full of the miracle of life. From two little fish in a sack we graduated, of course, to four goldfish in a one-gallon tank, and so on, up to thirty-two tropical fish in a forty-gallon tank, which was where we were when the boys left home for college.

I then became the proprietor of the forty-gallon tank, which soon sprung a fatal leak, and keeper of the fish, for which I had to acquire a new tank, this one fifty gallons, with all the lights, valves, filters, pumps, and other accessories necessary to the establishment of a balanced ecosystem for tropical fish, as well as the recommended pharmacopoeia of vitamins, medicines, and tonics prescribed as essential to their virility and happiness.

I don't remember when or why I got out of tropicals and into kois, but in time the kois perished, one by one, and the long adventure ended, leaving me with a feeling of melancholy and failure, not to mention two hundred dollars worth of damp equipment.

So I regarded the two new goldfish with a cynical eye. Denny was still in bed. The children were out of sight. Now was my chance. I could simply dash them down the electric disposer and stop the cycle from starting all over again.

By the time Denny got up the fish were hanging up near the surface of the water in the peanut-butter jar. That meant they were low on oxygen. "You'll have to put the goldfish in something larger," I told her, "or they'll die."

She got out a large glazed Mexican bowl and filled it with water and put the goldfish in it.

"Just make sure," I told her, "that when the kids go home they take the goldfish with them."

They never left our house, of course. Our daughter-in-law phoned the next evening to thank us for taking care of the children and I asked my wife to tell her they forgot to take the goldfish home.

"What did she say about the goldfish?" I asked when she hung up.

"She said the children don't remember any goldfish. She thinks maybe we should leave well enough alone."

"What does that mean?"

"I suppose it means they're ours."

I thought maybe I'd just leave them in the Mexican bowl and let them run down, like windup toys; but two days later they were still swimming about, looking for something, whatever it is goldfish look for. I simply couldn't let them perish, as long as they were trying.

I went down to the garage and found the old one-gallon tank.

CHAPTER TWENTY-FOUR

I bought the tree house for my grandson, of course. He wasn't old enough to build his own, and I couldn't wait. I had always wanted a tree house when I was a boy, but there was never the right kind of a tree, or if there was, we always moved away. I didn't want that to happen to the kid.

Every child needs a retreat, a place where he can escape adult logic; where he can be alone to fantasize, to create his own universe, with himself at the center. A good tree house, I always thought, ought to be equipped with a spyglass, so its occupant could look out upon his realm and familiarize himself with its every detail.

Two men delivered the house one morning by truck. Like most things these days, it came unassembled, but it was said to be easy to assemble with instructions. I will say there seemed to be more pieces to it than I had imagined when I saw the model on the sales lot out in El Monte. Before I gave it up I counted seventy separate pieces of wood, and there were three cartons of nuts, bolts, and washers.

"You think we can put it up in a day?" I asked the driver.

"Well," he said, not sounding too sure, "you ought to. It's about a six-beer job."

They left it in the backyard under the deodars. It looked like something blown down by a cyclone. I wondered where to begin. The sensible thing, I decided, would be to start with the first beer.

I had asked our two sons to come over in the afternoon to help, so I did nothing until they showed up. Then we moved all the parts down to the second level above the canyon. I wanted the tree house to have a good view.

I must explain that the house is not assembled in a tree, but sits up on wooden legs, so that its floor is six or seven feet above ground. It is a tree house without a tree, but it does have a slide, so you can come out the door and slide to the ground, and also a fireman's pole; and, suspended below the house, a glider and a swing.

Our sons are good with their hands, and the thing seemed to move right along. But we made a mistake or two and had to back-track, and when dark fell we had nothing but the supporting structure in place, with the slide and the swing. The house itself was still in sections, leaning against the sundial. The truck driver had been right. We were only half finished, but among us we had only drunk three beers.

The next day was Sunday and we might have finished the job, but both of my sons had other obligations. In the morning I went down to the site and looked it over. I knew I could never finish it by myself. I sat in the swing to think, and the next thing I knew I was swinging. Gradually, without realizing it, I gained momentum. Higher and higher I went, feet flying up against the sky. At last I slowed to a stop. I heard a woman's laugh and turned around. The Millers had walked up the hill to their mailbox and were looking down at me from the road.

"It's for the grandchildren," I said.

"Of course," said Mrs. Miller.

One weekend after the tree house was built we had the grand-children over, and I became more inclined than ever to believe that boys and girls are not the same.

Neither the feminists nor the psychologists in their camp have persuaded me that boys and girls are the same kind of people inside their heads, and that little girls would behave exactly like their brothers, unless we taught them not to.

What got me thinking about it again was an incident that occurred about six o'clock on Sunday morning, not long after the sun was up and I had become vaguely aware that a new day was on us.

"Grampa," said my granddaughter in my ear.

I don't much like being called Grampa. If I have to be given a new familiar name, simply because one of our sons has seen fit to have children of his own, I would prefer to be called Grandfather, or Jack. I don't see why having grand-children should deprive a man of his dignity.

"What do you want?" I asked, sure that whatever she wanted, it most probably should be referred to my wife, who was still asleep.

"Will you put this flower in my hair?"

She held out a plastic daisy, white and blue, and some kind of hairpin. As I had foreseen, it was a task for my wife; but my granddaughter's eyes were in their appealing phase, soft and helpless, and I thought, "Oh, what the hell."

I sat on the edge of the bed in my pajamas and pinned the flower in her hair. It wasn't a very good job. The daisy seemed to dangle, rather than float upright, but I doubted I could do any better.

"There you are," I said, and she trotted off, looking innocent as the morning; but it had been my experience that a girl who sets out with a flower in her hair, like a badge of good intentions, can do a lot of mischief.

In a moment I heard her talking with her brother. The

troops were up and restive, and one of us would have to get up too, and take over the bridge. I picked up a sock and put it on.

My granddaughter returned. She was holding a clutch of articles between her hands, the way you hold a wet kitten, and pushed it toward me. It turned out to be her shoes and socks. She wanted me to put them on. I looked at my wife, hoping she was awake. If she was, she wasn't letting on. Her head was under the pillow.

"Oh, all right," I said, and took the shoes and socks. I couldn't remember that I had ever put a small girl's shoes and socks on, not having had any daughters, but I assumed it wouldn't be a lot harder than putting on a boy's. That didn't turn out to be true.

I tried to put a sock on, but it seemed to be the wrong size. Then I saw why. She was squiggling her foot ever so little, not enough to appear openly uncooperative, but enough to frustrate operations.

"Keep your foot still," I said sternly. Her face clouded, but her foot went limp. In less than five minutes I had her shod. The feminists can say what they like, but it is harder to put a little girl's shoes and socks on than a little boy's, and I think it's congenital.

She skipped off and my grandson appeared in the doorway. He had dressed himself, being six, and I noticed that he had a rather wicked-looking pirate knife stuck under his belt. I hoped it was made of rubber.

"Can I play in the tree house," he asked, "Grampa?"

"Yes, of course," I said, thinking that if I worked with him on it I could get him to say Grandfather or Jack. "That's what it's for."

My wife's eyes were open. I think she knew the first wave had broken, and that there would be a lull. I told her about having to pin the daisy in her granddaughter's hair while her grandson armed himself with a knife and went out to play. "Why do you think she wanted to start the day with a flower in her hair?" I asked.

"I imagine it's something she got from her mother," she said.

"You mean heredity?"

"No. It's something her mother taught her."

"I don't believe it," I said. "It's in her genes, or hormones, or whatever it is."

She put her head back under the pillow.

I was thinking of getting dressed when a startling sound came from the living room. It was a rapid series of clicking sounds, like beans being spilled on the kitchen floor. I hurried out, baffled and alarmed. She was standing on our newly restored hardwood floor in a pool of spilled pearls.

"My pearls broke."

"I see."

"Why do you only have one sock on?"

"Because," I said, knowing I was being diverted from the pearls, "you've kept me so busy I haven't had time to put the other one on."

"I'm going out to play in the tree house," she said.

She went, without her pearls but with her flower, to see what she could do, I expect, to exasperate her brother.

I tell you, they're different.

Not long after making that discovery I took my granddaughter to a neighborhood Christmas party at the playground on our hill, and though there were a few exasperating moments, I think we both came away with the Yuletide spirit.

It was unusual for me to succumb to the sentiment so early in the season. I consider myself fairly sophisticated, if not cynical. I not only don't believe in Santa Claus, I doubt the wisdom of encouraging children to believe in Santa Claus.

The brighter ones soon see through the old fraud anyway, and then are obliged to suffer through that painful period when they know their parents aren't telling them the truth, but their parents don't know they know.

Also, for the first few weeks of the season I am usually armored against the signals that trip the Christmas emotional apparatus inside us all. My defense mechanism, which might be called the Humbug Response, goes into action. I deplore the commercialization; I am surfeited with the carols oozing out of every wall; I resist the pressure to send Christmas cards, buy presents, be jolly.

But sooner or later, usually on Christmas Eve, it reaches me. A bar of "Silent Night" catches me in an unguarded moment; a young woman hurries into an elevator with her arms full of packages, her face flushed; there are pictures in the paper of snow-covered towns in Maine; the Christmas cards pile up on the bar. And suddenly old Scrooge turns into a sugarplum.

I wasn't yet a sugarplum, though, when Adriana and I set out for the party. Denny and I had taken her and her brother in for the night and I had thought we would all go to the party. But my wife had a cold and sounded like a frog, and our grandson decided at the last minute to exercise his negative power.

"Will Santa Claus be there?" he asked.

"I think so," I said, waffling.

"I saw Santa Claus already," he said.

I suspected he knew already.

"Will there be any reindeer?" he asked.

"No. I don't think so. Not real ones, anyway."

"I don't want to go."

Adriana and I set out by ourselves. She climbed into the front seat and crawled over to the passenger side and when I started the engine the seat-belt buzzer buzzed. I started to fasten her seat belt but she climbed over the seat and sat in the rear. I couldn't coax her back.

It was a stormy night. An hour earlier the sky had been ripped by lightning and thunder, and it was dark and wet when I drove over the narrow streets of Mount Washington in search of the playground.

I made what I thought was the proper turn, but a minute later I knew it wasn't. The street grew narrower and more serpentine and tailed off in a series of dead ends, like the frayed end of a string. I turned around and went back and started out again, making the same wrong turn, and this time ending up at the bottom of the hill.

In the back seat my passenger was singing and talking to herself, obviously unaware that she was in the hands of a man who was lost. I was irritated. I knew Mount Washington like the palm of my hand. I started back up the hill and when I was quite sure I was lost again I suddenly came out at the playground.

We parked and walked across the wet street toward the clubhouse. Inside they were singing "Silent Night," the neighborhood's voices, young and old, true and vagrant. The sound seemed almost touchable in the rainy night. ". . . all is calm, all is bright . . ." I felt a sudden warmth, a tightening of the throat. "Oh, come on," I told myself. "You act like Pavlov's dog."

There was a lighted Christmas tree in the hall and the people were sitting on folding chairs with most of the children on the floor. They finished "Silent Night" and went into "Jingle Bells." We stood at one side and listened. My granddaughter held my hand. She was wearing a red and green coat with a fur-lined hood. Her face was pink and her eyes were very wide. She made me think of Dickens. When you think of Dickens, you are beginning to crumble.

She stood as still as a bell on the tree. We had come out

of a dark wet night into this room full of strange people and colored lights and songs that were already dyed into her memory from two Christmases past. It was all being stored away in her unconscious, I knew, and years later, all her life, when suddenly she responded to some signal—perhaps a bar of "Silent Night" oozing from the wall—this moment would reverberate. She would never remember it consciously, but it would be there, a part of every Christmas yet to come.

"Was there any reindeer?" my grandson asked when we got home.

"No," I said. "There weren't any reindeer."

"Was Santa Claus there?"

It wasn't my grandson who asked. It was my wife. It doesn't make any difference how long you live with them. You never really know what they believe in.

CHAPTER TWENTY-FIVE

I needn't have worried about not knowing spring had come. Our grandchildren spent the weekend with us, which got me outdoors, to keep an eye on them, and it was obviously spring.

I couldn't leave them unguarded for long in our backyard, since it is not fenced in, except for the dog yard, and it drops off into a steep canyon, thick with scrub and poison oak and inhabited by all sorts of small wild creatures.

The birds were busy. Scrub jays, mockingbirds, towhees, doves, finches. But no hummingbirds. I kept an eye on my feeder, which they had ignored so far that year, but nothing happened.

As long as I had to stay outdoors I decided I might as well do something useful. I got a hammer and a concrete nail and started to drive the nail into the cement-block wall around my wife's private garden. I had put low-voltage floodlights in the garden and the transformer had to be hung above the ground. The wall seemed a good place.

"What are you doing?" Cristophe asked.

"I'm hammering this nail into this wall," I said.

It was hard going. My blows drove the nail in visibly for a few minutes, but then it seemed to meet some harder resistance.

"Why?" he asked.

I stopped to wipe my forehead and rest. I was not really in shape to be driving nails into concrete, and I realized there was a possibility I might have a heart attack.

"To hang this transformer on," I said.

"What's that?"

I considered my chances of explaining a transformer to a six-year-old boy, especially since I didn't understand it myself. Fortunately I was rescued from this predicament by a lizard that skittered over the wall and took shelter in some plants.

"A yizzard!" the boy screamed.

"Lizard," I said. "L. L as in lichee nut."

"Yizzard!" he screamed again, which set his sister to screaming too, though she couldn't even say yizzard yet. I wondered why Cristophe couldn't say his L's. His mother had a French accent, of course, but L wasn't one of her problems.

"Do yizzards bite?" he asked.

"Yes, but it doesn't hurt."

"I think I'll catch a bird," he said.

"Good," I said, wanting to get on with my nail. "Go catch a bird."

He was soon at the edge of the canyon, stalking birds. I knew I ought to call him back. If he fell down the canyon he might be eaten by birds and small mammals and reptiles before we could find him. It had always worried us when we first moved into the house. Our boys were then the age our grandchildren are now; but they never fell, and we realized we had been overprotective. It was a word that was just then coming into vogue, and we hadn't known it was bad.

I decided to go to the garage and get a heavier hammer. I had been hitting the nail for half an hour and wasn't getting anywhere. To get to the garage you have to go through the dog yard. The grandchildren followed me to the gate. "Listen," I said sternly. "Don't open this gate. The dog will get out. You understand?"

They nodded, but the girl looked mischievous. I was no sooner in the garage than I heard a shout: "She yet the dog out!"

I ran out too late. Fleetwood Pugsley was not only out, but gone. Adriana looked guilty. She had done it deliberately. I hated to paddle her, so near to her birthday. I wasn't sure a grandfather had the authority. I wasn't sure, either, that it would do her any good. But I thought it might do me some good, and it did.

It was Sunday afternoon before their mother and father arrived to pick them up. I was still working on the nail, hammering at it for five minutes or so and resting half an hour, so as not to have a heart attack.

"Here," Doug said, "let me try."

He gave the nail a few whacks. It resisted him as it had me. Then suddenly it began to go in, and in a minute the job was done.

"Well," I pointed out, "I guess I practically had it licked, and you just gave it the coup de grace."

Suddenly Cristophe screamed. It was not merely a theatrical scream to draw attention to some minor wound. It was real. We ran to him.

"A bee bit me!" he whimpered, holding out one hand.

A bee had lit on the palm of his hand, he explained later, and he had closed his hand, thinking to capture it, evidently on the theory that a bee in the hand is worth a bird in the bush.

"I guess we never told him bees sting," Doug said. "Oh, well, he knows now."

It seemed incredible to me that a father had not told a five-year-old son that bees sting. But then of course you can't tell them everything. Sometimes you just have to wait until they get stung.

I wondered if there was anything I never explained to my own children. The only things I could think of offhand were sex and transformers.

Oh well, they know now.

CHAPTER TWENTY-SIX

An application for renewal of my driver's license came in the mail, reminding me that my current license would expire on my birthday, and that it could be renewed at any time up until then. I must fill out the enclosed application and present it at the nearest office of the Department of Motor Vehicles.

It seemed like more than a minor event. For one thing, it meant I was four years older. Four years had passed since I had last stood in line with the other applicants, answered that long list of multiple-choice questions on traffic laws, had my eyes examined and my picture taken and walked out with the most precious privilege the state of California could confer except the vote itself.

I felt a tremor of anxiety. The older we get, the further we get away from the need to pass tests, except those our doctors give us. If I applied on or before my birthday, most likely I wouldn't have to take an actual driving test; but still it was going to be an ordeal. My eyes weren't getting any sharper. So far I had never had a license restricting me to driving with glasses, but the time might have come. I was already into my third set of bifocals.

I waited till my birthday and then drove out to the DMV in Hollywood. I showed my card to a man at the information window.

"Get in the typing line," he said.

The typing line was thirty feet long. Cursing bureaucracy, I fell in at the rear. In exactly thirty minutes I reached the typist.

She was polite and efficient. She took $3.25 from me, typed out my papers, handed me the long test form and told me to fill it out and get in line 3 or 5.

There were thirty-six questions on the test, each with three answers, only one of which was correct. I filled it out quickly but carefully. As usual, when I didn't know the law, I checked the answer that seemed the most sensible. Over the years, I have found that the state of California is almost as sensible as I am.

I got in line 5. Even from the end of the line I could read the eye chart with my glasses. I tried it with my glasses off. I could read it with my right eye, but not with my left. The little tremor came back. It was going to be a milestone in my life. I was going to fail the eye test.

There was time enough to memorize the chart with my glasses on. I decided against it. It wasn't honest. Besides, the examiner would probably make me read a line backward and I'd be exposed as a cheat.

My turn came at last. To my annoyance, I was nervous. Ridiculous. I wasn't a schoolboy, after all. I was a mature man, a citizen in good standing and an excellent driver, despite the fact that every time Jacqueline rode with me she was continually gasping and clutching at her breast. It bothered me, even though I knew it was pure Gallic theatricality.

The examiner ran his eye down both sides of my test sheet. I had made two errors. Both of them, I saw, were on bad laws which I trusted would be corrected in due time.

The examiner held a card in front of my left eye and asked me to read the last line of the chart. It was a snap. He covered my right eye. A blur.

"You can't read it?"

"Nothing."

He moved me over to a machine with an eyepiece and gave me a series of what I took to be peripheral vision and depth-perception tests.

"Well," he said, "you passed. But just barely."

At last I stood at the red line in front of the camera. "Look at the red light," said the young woman behind the camera, "and smile." A light flashed.

She handed me my temporary license and told me my renewal would come along in the mail within sixty days.

"Happy birthday," she said.

How nice of her, I thought. She had noticed.

I walked out into the sunlight, my sharp eyes perceiving the depths, observing the periphery. My tremor was gone. My step was bouncy. I was a full citizen, renewed and unrestricted, in the greatest state of the nation.

All the same, I put my glasses on to drive home.

Not long after I was thus certified as a functioning member of society, I was called into service on a mission of importance.

I decided to wear gray slacks and a blue blazer with a pink button-down shirt and navy blue tie. It was very important, I had always thought, what one wore the first day of school.

Of course it wasn't *my* first day of school, but my grandson's. He was going into the first grade. Something had come up that made it impossible for his mother or father to take him, and I was drafted.

When I got to Jacqueline's house she had a cup of coffee waiting for me. The schoolboy was ready. He was wearing a light blue mock turtleneck and blue slacks with a Spiderman belt buckle and red sneakers. His lunch pail was blue.

"I think we'll walk," I said, "instead of taking the car."

It was cool and overcast as we walked down the shady street to the boulevard. Dogs barked at us, not angry; yellow flowers tumbled to the sidewalk from a yard; a gardener was out working and there was a smell of cut grass. We came to a corner where two main streets converged and angled off. I wasn't sure which one to take. "Do we go this way or that way?" I asked.

"That way," he said.

"Are you sure?"

"I'm sure, but I'm not *very* sure."

That seemed about the right attitude to begin school with. We walked on a block or two. "My arm's tired," he said. "This lunch pail's too heavy."

"Switch it to the other arm," I said.

We passed a court with a small sign stuck in the lawn. "What's that sign say?" he asked. "DON'T WALK"?

"No. It says VISITORS PARK OUTSIDE." He *did* have a lot to learn.

"You know what I want?" he said. "A six-million-dollar man."

"Six million dollars is too much."

"He doesn't cost that much. That's his name."

It was small talk, to keep our minds off the unknown.

We walked past the school playground where children of various sizes and colors were already gathering in tentative groups.

"Is that Room 8?" he asked.

"No. That's outdoors. Room 8 is a room."

The school was green stucco, one story, with a little cupola. A small but opulent fig tree had scattered large brown leaves on the lawn. We turned up a red brick walk to the entrance and walked past a busy office and down an arcade by an inner courtyard. The slip of paper in my pocket said Cristophe was to report at nine o'clock to Mrs. Goode in

Room 8. It was eight-forty-five. A young woman with a clip-board headed us off.

"We're looking for Room 8," I told her.

"I'm Mrs. Goode," she said. "I am Room 8."

I wasn't doing too well. I had told him Room 8 had to be a room, not a playground, and now it had turned out to be a person.

"I can show him the room," she said pleasantly, firm but not awesome, "and then take him down to the play-ground. The classes will be gathering on the playground at nine o'clock."

"I guess I'm not needed," I said. "I'm the grandfather."

I could almost hear her thinking. *Oh dear. Another grandfather. I hope he won't be difficult.* She looked down at her new pupil. He was bearing up, but I thought his eyes were glassy.

"You can stay if you like," she said to me. "Would you like to see the room?"

The room was neat and cheerful. A wallboard was covered with watercolors of butterflies, ice cream cones, sail-boats, and other quite nice things. A large paper sign was lettered in crayon: TODAY IS TUESDAY. WE ARE IN ROOM 8. WE WILL HAVE FUN.

Mrs. Goode said we might go on down to the playground and she'd be along. There were more children on the play-ground now, and teachers and a few parents. We stood off to one side, looking nonchalant.

A woman with a clipboard hurried up to me. "Are you Mr. Shapiro?" she asked.

"No," I said. "I'm a grandfather."

The bell rang.

A woman at the top of the walk, on the bank between the playground and the schoolhouse, called out over a red bullhorn: "Boys and girls! Go *across* the playground and line up with your classes!"

We found Mrs. Goode. Her class was small, five boys and five girls, or thereabouts. They were forming a line, more or less. She took Cristophe's hand and put him in behind a boy in a green football jersey with the number 12 on the front. Joe Namath.

"You can stand here behind Fred," said Mrs. Goode.

In a minute they all marched off, up the bank to the schoolhouse and through the door. I watched until it had swallowed the last one and the playground was deserted.

He was on his way. Out into the world. Beginning his great adventure. I was grateful to the winds of chance that had blown my way and let me lead him to this door. I stood on the empty and silent playground for a minute, filling it with the faces and voices of my own schooldays. I had forgotten my first day. But I would always remember his.

Walking back to the house I stopped a moment to admire a sunflower plant beside the sidewalk. There were four large flowers, three turned rather toward the south, I thought, the other one north. Was it true that sunflowers turned toward the sun as it moved across the sky? But the sun wasn't out this morning. Was that why they faced the wrong way? Were they confused?

That was one of the wonderful things about life, I thought, as I walked on. One always had so much to learn.

CHAPTER TWENTY-SEVEN

It was Jacqueline's love of French cheese that led to her employment as a cheese importer's representative in gourmet grocery stores, and indirectly to her first contact with the French-speaking community of Los Angeles.

This in turn led to a situation in which I was able to give her some advice and support, and which, I believe, ultimately gave the two of us a heightened respect and affection for each other.

She had been asked by a group of French-speaking teachers to give a talk on cheeses at one of their meetings, speaking in French, of course, and she had accepted, only to regret it at once.

As the day grew near she became sick with anxiety. She had never before talked to a group larger than her family, afraid she would be too nervous to utter a sound. She simply could not go through with it.

"But it ought to be a piece of cake," I told her. "You'll be speaking in French, after all."

"Zat is z'problem," she said. "Zey are all teachers of French and I am just a poor uneducated little girl from Tours."

I am no judge of the quality of her French, of course, but I had heard that Touraine French was the purest French

of all, and even if she hadn't been at the top of her class at
the Lycée Choiseul, she ought to be able to give a little talk
on cheeses without embarrassing herself.

"Mr. Smith," she said, "I cannot do it. I will say I am
sick."

"No," I said. "You can't do that. You have committed
yourself, and you must do it."

"You are right," she agreed wretchedly.

"Would it help," I asked, "if I went with you? You can
pretend you're just talking to me."

"You would do zat?"

Her apprehension, I noticed, had brought back her z's.

"If you like," I said.

Actually, I was well qualified to help her. I too had
once been pathologically afraid of talking before groups, but
I had had to do it, and in time had overcome my fear.

"You simply tell them a funny story to begin with," I
advised, "and make them laugh, and they will be your friends
from then on. Believe me."

"What if zey do not laugh?"

"They will laugh," I said, though I knew they were un-
predictable, and might not.

I tried to make her see that she was a very charming
and amusing woman, with a gift for telling funny stories. I
remembered how funny it had seemed to me when she told the
story of her trip to Baja with her three friends.

"You can tell a funny story about *me,* if you like," I
said. "You must know one or two."

"You would not mind?"

"Of course not. Not if it will put you at ease."

It was an all-day meeting at a school in the elegant old
Hancock Park neighborhood, and my daughter-in-law could
hardly have been more intimidated than I was. There were

perhaps 150 others present, a rather chic and sophisticated-looking crowd, I thought, and even the casual conversation in the hallways was limited to French. The morning seminar was on various topics of interest to the French community, and Jacqueline was on the program to follow a writer who discussed her most recent cookbook. I could not understand a word the cookbook author said, but I could sense her skill, and her audience was obviously entranced.

All this time my daughter-in-law sat beside me, twisting a handkerchief in her hands and expelling a series of taut little sighs.

The applause for her predecessor died out. Her time had come. She rose and walked to the podium. Joan of Arc, walking to the stake. I am familiar with the silence that falls between one's introduction and one's opening words. It is awesome. The introduction was over. She stood alone before her silent audience.

She began. I was surprised at the measure of my own anxiety. I was almost glad it was Jacqueline up there, not me. My chivalry was gone. She had managed to get started, and the telltale signs of nervousness were there. But she flew on, stalling for a terrifying moment, like an old biplane at a flying circus, then spinning out and leveling off, only to stall again.

But something was happening. A scattering of laughter, tentative. Then another. Then it was louder and intermittent. Finally, as my daughter-in-law waxed on, warming to her story, whatever it was, the laughter erupted. The hilarity was genuine.

I was sitting at the back, and faces turned toward me, laughing, their eyes searching me out as my daughter-in-law sailed on. They wanted to share their delight with the lucky father-in-law of such a treasure. It was contagious. I was laughing too, though I hadn't the slightest idea what she was saying.

The story ended. The laughter subsided. But she had weathered her fright. Now she was coasting; I could tell. She finished quite gracefully, and left the podium to what sounded like sincere applause.

"You were great!" I told her afterward. "Just great! What were you telling them, anyway, that was so funny?"

"Oh, Mr. Smith," she said, "I hope you will forgive me."

"Forgive you? For what? I'm *proud* of you."

"Mr. Smith, I tell zem the story about how you cannot eat the little birds with their little heads and their little feet and you think the cognac is wine and you get *smash* and pour cognac on the table at my wedding breakfast."

So I had helped her after all.

"I'll tell you what," I said as I drove her home. "I'll forget you ever told that story if you forget it ever happened."

"Mr. Smith," she said, "it's a deal."

"By the way," I said, "now that we're such good friends, you don't have to call me Mr. Smith any more."

"Mr. Smith," she said, "I cannot help it. It is the way I am brought up. The fazher-in-law must be treated with respect. To me you will always be Mr. Smith."

Looking at it that way, I rather liked the idea.

CHAPTER TWENTY-EIGHT

Curt has a sense of theater, and sometimes he enjoys breaking the most exciting news in an oblique or offhand manner, so that one does not get it directly, and the effect, when it does come through, is all the greater.

Late one afternoon he phoned to ask me about a business matter, and when we had finished with that he said, "Oh, there's something else."

"Yes?"

"Gail's in labor."

My response was a prolonged silence. My clock was not set for that revelation. It was premature. The baby had not been expected for another ten days, and babies in my family had always been on time, or late.

The way he had broken the news reminded me of a day in April thirty-two years earlier, when a corporal named Jones sauntered into a Dallas hut on Maui, where our division was recuperating after Iwo Jima, and said casually, "You guys hear the news? Truman's President."

First, one had to think who Truman was. Then one had to wonder how Truman could suddenly be President. Only then did the shocking truth sink in. Roosevelt, somehow, was dead.

I remembered also that only the previous September Curt had invited all of us out to dinner, including the Paoluccis and Bernadette, and Douglas and Jacqueline and the two children. The scene he had chosen was rather an expensive restaurant at the Marina, and my feeling that he was being frightfully extravagant was heightened when he ordered Mumm's champagne. I had raised him to believe that a good California champagne was suitable for any occasion.

By no amount of wheedling could he be induced to disclose the reason for this festive gathering before he was ready. Only when he stood up, at last, champagne glass in hand, did the explanation come, and even then it was indirect.

I had guessed, by then, that he had been given a substantial raise, if not actually elevated to chairman of the board. At UCLA he had changed his major to environmental geography after the war, and then had done a graduate year in that field and was now employed as an environmentalist with a large utility company.

Gail had been steadily employed in physical therapy after graduating, and their combined incomes had given them a level of affluence that my wife and I could only have dreamed of when we were their age. Perhaps, I guessed, he was going to announce that they had bought a house in Bel-Air, or at least a yacht.

We all fell silent at the table. Even the children sensed that something exciting was about to be said, and turned their faces expectantly toward their uncle.

"Cristophe and Adriana," he said momentously, smiling down at the two children, now enchanted by the sound of their own names, "are going to have a cousin."

Mary Ann Paolucci was seated at my right. She looked at me, and I watched her face turn from uncertainty to comprehension to joy. She and Bernie Paolucci had long made it clear that they were ready for such an event.

I remembered the lines from Kahlil Gibran, which of course had been read into their wedding ceremony at their request, that they were the bows from which their children, like arrows, would be sent forth.

Their first arrow was in flight.

"It's probably a false alarm," I told Curt over the phone. Ten days early wasn't like the Smiths. But somewhat after five o'clock he called back to say that he and Gail were leaving for the hospital. I was about to advise against this, pointing out that it was a bad hour for traffic; but I realized they were dealing with an urgency that was oblivious to such inauspicious factors.

Denny and I decided not to go to the hospital. We knew the Paoluccis would be there, and one set of grandparents ought to be enough. But we spent a restive night.

Curt phoned at five o'clock in the morning. The delivery had been made. It was a girl, and her name was Alison Paolucci Smith.

For a moment I indulged myself in the notion that I had been influential in the choice of that name, remembering my suggestion that they preserve Gail's maiden name as a middle name for the child, whatever its sex. But it was probably only a coincidence. I couldn't remember that either of my daughters-in-law had ever taken any advice of mine, and certainly not in a matter as serious as naming a baby.

"And now," I thought, counting on my fingers, "there are nine of us."

I soon found out what my function was to be in greeting this new member of the family. All of us gathered that evening at the hospital in Santa Monica to see the principals, and since small children are not allowed in maternity wards, it was decided that I should wait in the downstairs lobby with the cousins.

I might have managed it with poise, I believe, except that someone else had left two small children down below, without a guardian. I found myself suddenly trying to manage four children, instead of two, and quickly discovered that the amount of energy and mischief released by four children is a quantum jump over the amount released by two.

The critical point came when Adriana, who had proposed a game of hide-and-seek, not only found a place to hide from the two strange children, but also from me. My annoyance soon turned to alarm. I could find her nowhere.

"Where is she?" I demanded of her brother.

"She's in the praying room," he said.

"She's in the what?"

He showed me. She had hidden in the dimly lighted chapel off the lobby, from which I furtively retrieved her. I was about to ask my grandson where he had picked up that extraordinary phrase "praying room" when the hospital security officer appeared, looking every inch an authority figure in his blue uniform and leather harness.

"Here now!" he barked. "Stop that noise!" There was no chuckle in his voice and no friendly twinkle in the reproachful glance he sent my way.

"I'm only responsible for two of them," I pointed out.

"They'll have to be quiet," he said, making it plain that he considered me responsible for the whole lot. I was glad he hadn't come along while my granddaughter was hiding in the praying room.

Finally Doug came down in the elevator and took over and I went up to see my new granddaughter through a window. Alison Paolucci Smith. She looked as if she'd been in a fight and lost the first round. She also looked like a winner. I decided to call her Lucci.

The others moved down the corridor to talk to a nurse, and for a moment I was alone with my granddaughter. I blew her a kiss through the window.

It seemed like a good time to spend one.

ABOUT THE AUTHOR

Jack Smith is a popular columnist for the *Los Angeles Times*, the author of several books, and a contributor to such national magazines as *Westways, Travel & Leisure, Holiday,* the *Ladies' Home Journal,* and *The Saturday Evening Post.* He began his career as a sports writer for the Bakersfield *Californian,* and subsequently worked on the *Honolulu Advertiser,* the *Sacramento Union,* the *San Diego Journal,* the *Los Angeles Daily News,* and the *Los Angeles Herald-Express.* During World War II he joined the U.S. Marine Corps and served as a Marine combat correspondent in the battle of Iwo Jima. He and his wife live on Mt. Washington, near the center of Los Angeles, and own a Mexican house on the Pacific Ocean in Baja California, the building of which was the subject of his highly acclaimed hilarious adventure, *God and Mr. Gomez.*